I0145399

PASSPORT

Citizen of the Kingdom of God

By Pastor Thornton Bell Sr.

THE KINGDOM OF GOD PASSPORT

By Pastor Thornton Bell Sr.

Copyright © 2007 by Pastor Thornton Bell

All scripture references are from the Authorized King James Version of the Bible

All Rights Reserved. No part of this publication may be reproduced, stored in retrieval systems, or transmitted in any form or by any means electronic, mechanical, photocopying, recording, or otherwise, without the prior written permission of the Author.

Published By:
Thornton Bell –
IMPACT NOW Ministries
2003 Meadows Drive
Birmingham, Alabama 35235
(205) 655-6708

ISBN - 978-0-6151-6358-1
Printed in the United States of America
www.lulu.com

PLEASE COMPLETE IN INK OR PENCIL AS YOU DESIRE:

Name:

_____

Address:

_____

Telephone:

_____

Next of Kin:

_____

If lost or in case of emergency, please contact the following minister:

_____

Forward

In Mark 16:15 -18, Jesus tells His disciples to go out into the world and preach the gospel. This call to be witnesses of the Gospel of Jesus continues to all believers today. However, in order to leave our borders and become witnesses to other nations, we must have a passport. The *Kingdom of God Passport* serves as a practical reminder for all believers to get busy, get out, and witness as commanded. It also contains valuable information to help the believer in his/her witness. Because believers are citizens of another kingdom, we should carry our *Kingdom of God Passport* at all times.

This is an excellent memory jogger and study diary for all believers. Included is a section for keeping track of some of your most memorable experiences in Christ. It also provides an excellent teaching instrument for new converts and those who are beginning to enjoy witnessing for Christ. You must get yours today. Remember; do not be ashamed to carry it at all times.

Pastor Thornton Bell

Much credit for this journal belongs to Pastor and Prophetess Mattie J. Bass and Apostle Andrew Wutawunashe for their sound teaching and ideas. We give all glory to God, Jesus, and the Holy Ghost

PASSPORT

THE KINGDOM OF GOD

PASSPORT
By virtue of the
Father, Son & Holy
Ghost

Type/ Category	Code of issuing state/code du pays emetteur	PASSPORT NO. / NO. DU PASSEPORT

Born Again   **Repentance**   **John 3:7**

Surname / Nom

—————————————

Given Names / Nationalite'

————————————————————

PASTE
YOUR
PICTURE
HERE

Date of Birth / Date de naissance
(born again date)

——————————

Sex / Sexe   Place of birth / Lu de naissance

——————   ———————/————————/————————

Date of issue / Date de'
delivrance

Date of expiration /
Date de' expiration

Eternal Life

Authority / Autorite'
Matthew 28:18

Amendments
/
Modifications

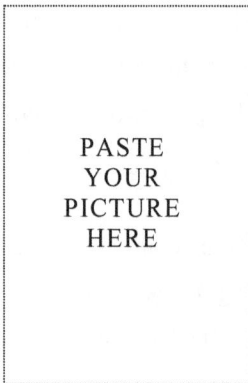

4

The Word of God,
the Christ,
the Son of the living God,
of the Kingdom of God
hereby commands all whom it may concern to permit the citizen /
national of the Kingdom of God named herein to pass
without delay or hindrance and in case of need to
give all lawful aid and protection

<u>Mark 16:15-23</u>

15   *And he said unto them, Go ye into all the world, and preach the gospel to every creature.*

16   *He that believeth and is baptized shall be saved; but he that believeth not shall be damned.*

17   *And these signs shall follow them that believe; In my name shall they cast out devils; they shall speak with new tongues;*

18   *They shall take up serpents; and if they drink any deadly thing, it shall not hurt them; they shall lay hands on the sick, and they shall recover.*

The Blood Of Jesus

SIGNATURE OF BEARER / SIGNATURE DU TITULAIRE

NOT VALID UNTIL SIGNED

5

1   The Way of Salvation

(a)   The Problem –

Why do we need salvation?   Ans.:   People are born under the curse of **sin, judgment, death, and oppression**.

> *Important biblical references,* Romans *3:2; Romans 6:2; Romans 5:12; and Revelation 20:11-15.*

> **Romans 3:23;** For all have sinned, and come short of the glory of God;
> **Romans 6:23;** For the wages of sin is death; but the gift of God is eternal life through Jesus Christ our Lord.
> **Romans 5:12;** Wherefore, as by one man sin entered into the world, and death by sin; and so death passed upon all men, for that all have sinned:
> **Revelation 20:11;** And I saw a great white throne, and him that sat on it, from whose face the earth and the heaven fled away; and there was found no place for them. **12** And I saw the dead, small and great, stand before God; and the books were opened: and another book was opened, which is the book of life: and the dead were judged out of those things which were written in the books, according to their works. **13** And the sea gave up the dead which were in it; and death and hell delivered up the dead which were in them: and they were judged every man according to their works. **14** And death and hell were cast into the lake of fire. This is the second death. **15** And whosoever was not found written in the book of life was cast into the lake of fire.

6

(b) The Solution –

There is a way out. God provided in His Son Jesus Christ as the *only* way to be saved and made free from the bondages of **sin, judgment, death,** and **oppression:**

Important biblical references, Romans 5:8; Isaiah 53:4-6; John 14:6; 1 John 3:8; Acts 4:12.

> **Romans 5: 8;** But God commendeth his love toward us, in that, while we were yet sinners, Christ died for us.

> **Isaiah 53:4;** Surely he hath borne our griefs, and carried our sorrows: yet we did esteem him stricken, smitten of God, and afflicted. **5** But he was wounded for our transgressions, he was bruised for our iniquities: the chastisement of our peace was upon him; and with his stripes we are healed. **6** All we like sheep have gone astray; we have turned every one to his own way; and the LORD hath laid on him the iniquity of us all.

> **John 14:6;** Jesus saith unto him, I am the way, the truth, and the life: no man cometh unto the Father, but by me.

> **1 John 3:8;** He that committeth sin is of the devil; for the devil sinneth from the beginning. For this purpose the Son of God was manifested, that he might destroy the works of the devil.

> **Acts 4:12;** Neither is there salvation in any other: for there is none other name under heaven given among men, whereby we must be saved.

(c) What Must I Do?

What happens when you believe in Jesus and what did Jesus do for you when He suffered and died on the cross? What happens when you decided to repent of your sins and receive the risen **JESUS** as you Christ, Lord and savoir?

Answer:

> *If you mean it, you receive eternal life. You receive Him by believing, repenting and calling on His name.*

> **John 3:16;** For God so loved the world, that he gave his only begotten Son, that whosoever believeth in him should not perish, but have everlasting life

> **2Corinthians. 7:10;** For godly sorrow worketh repentance to salvation not to be repented of: but the sorrow of the world worketh death.

> **Romans 10:9-13;** That if thou shalt confess with thy mouth the Lord Jesus, and shalt believe in thine heart that God hath raised him from the dead, thou shalt be saved. **10** For with the heart man believeth unto righteousness; and with the mouth confession is made unto salvation. **11** For the scripture saith, Whosoever believeth on him shall not be ashamed. **12** For there is no difference between the Jew and the Greek: for the same Lord over all is rich unto all that call upon him. **13** For whosoever shall call upon the name of the Lord shall be saved.

> **Isaiah 55:6-7;** Seek ye the LORD while he may be found, call ye upon him while he is near: **7** Let the wicked forsake his way, and the unrighteous man his thoughts: and let him return unto the LORD, and he will have mercy upon him; and to our God, for he will abundantly pardon.

8

IMPORTANT INFORMATION

... And, YES - Repentance is necessary.) Remember, God knows whether you truly believe in Jesus.

(d) Assurance:

You must know that your salvation is by *faith* (believing God's promises) and *faith* alone:

Important biblical reference are, Ephesians 2:8-9, 1John 5:11-13, John 6:37, and Titus 1:2.

> **Ephesians 2:8;** For by grace are ye saved through faith; and that not of yourselves: it is the gift of God: **9** Not of works, lest any man should boast.
>
> **1 John 5:11;** And this is the record, that God hath given to us eternal life, and this life is in his Son. **12** He that hath the Son hath life; and he that hath not the Son of God hath not life. **13** These things have I written unto you that believe on the name of the Son of God; that ye may know that ye have eternal life, and that ye may believe on the name of the Son of God.
>
> **John 6:37;** All that the Father giveth me shall come to me; and him that cometh to me I will in no wise cast out.
>
> **Titus 1:2;** In hope of eternal life, which God, that cannot lie, promised before the world began;

IMPORTANT INFORMATION

MEMORY VERSES: Romans 5:8; John 3:16; John 6:37

Romans 5:8 But God commendeth his love toward us, in that, while we were yet sinners, Christ died for us.

John 3:16 For God so loved the world, that he gave his only begotten Son, that whosoever believeth in him should not perish, but have everlasting life.

John 6:37 All that the Father giveth me shall come to me; and him that cometh to me I will in no wise cast out.

2. Benefits of Salvation

Here is what happens when you give your life to Christ.

(a) You Are Born Again:

The old person who was dead in sin is gone now, a new person in you is born again, you know a change has taken place, and you have become spiritually alive. Your old life of sin is in the past.

John 3:3; Jesus answered and said unto him, Verily, verily, I say unto thee, Except a man be born again, he cannot see the kingdom of God.
1 Peter 1:23; Being born again, not of corruptible seed, but of incorruptible, by the word of God, which liveth and abideth for ever.
Ephesians 2:1-2; **1** And you hath he quickened, who were dead in trespasses and sins; **2** Wherein in time past ye walked according to the course of this world, according to the prince of the power of the air, the spirit that now worketh in the children of disobedience:

(b) You Are A New Creature.

2 Corinthians 5:17; Therefore if any man be in Christ, he is a new creature: old things are passed away; behold, all things are become new.

John 1:12; But as many as received him, to them gave he power to become the sons of God, even to them that believe on his name:

11

IMPORTANT INFORMATION

Hebrews 8:12; For I will be merciful to their unrighteousness, and their sins and their iniquities will I remember no more.

1Peter 1:18-19; Forasmuch as ye know that ye were not redeemed with corruptible things, as silver and gold, from your vain conversation received by tradition from your fathers; **19** But with the precious blood of Christ, as of a lamb without blemish and without spot:

(c) *You Were Redeemed*

You are released from all of Satan's power - sin, sickness, oppression, poverty, and darkness, etc.

1Peter 1:18-19; Forasmuch as ye know that ye were not redeemed with corruptible things, as silver and gold, from your vain conversation received by tradition from your fathers; **19** But with the precious blood of Christ, as of a lamb without blemish and without spot:

Galatians 3:13-14; Christ hath redeemed us from the curse of the law, being made a curse for us: for it is written, Cursed is every one that hangeth on a tree: **14** That the blessing of Abraham might come on the Gentiles through Jesus Christ; that we might receive the promise of the Spirit through faith.

Isaiah 53:1-6; Who hath believed our report? and to whom is the arm of the LORD revealed? **2** For he shall grow up before him as a tender plant, and as a root out of a dry ground: he hath no form nor comeliness; and when we shall see him, there is no beauty that we should desire him. **3** He is despised and rejected of men; a man of sorrows, and acquainted with grief: and we hid as it were our faces from him; he was despised, and we esteemed him not. **4** Surely he hath borne our griefs, and carried our sorrows: yet we did esteem him stricken, smitten of God, and afflicted. **5** But he was wounded for our transgressions, he was bruised for our iniquities: the chastisement of our peace was upon him; and with his stripes we are healed. **6** All we like sheep have gone astray; we have turned every one to his own way; and the LORD hath laid on him the iniquity of us all.

1Peter 2:24; Who his own self bare our sins in his own body on the tree, that we, being dead to sins, should live unto righteousness: by whose stripes ye were healed.

2Cor.8:9; For ye know the grace of our Lord Jesus Christ, that, though he was rich, yet for your sakes he became poor, that ye through his poverty might be rich.

Colossians 1:13-14; Who hath delivered us from the power of darkness, and hath translated us into the kingdom of his dear Son: **14** In whom we have redemption through his blood, even the forgiveness of sins:

(d) *You Were Forgiven*

All of your sins are now forgiven. Go and sin no more.

Isaiah 1:18; Come now, and let us reason together, saith the LORD: though your sins be as scarlet, they shall be as white as snow; though they be red like crimson, they shall be as wool.

Hebrews 8:12; For I will be merciful to their unrighteousness, and their sins and their iniquities will I remember no more.

1John 1:9; If we confess our sins, he is faithful and just to forgive us our sins, and to cleanse us from all unrighteousness.

John 5:24; Verily, verily, I say unto you, He that heareth my word, and believeth on him that sent me, hath everlasting life, and shall not come into condemnation; but is passed from death unto life.

You received Christ's righteousness. You can prove it by living right.

2Corinthians 5:21; For he hath made him to be sin for us, who knew no sin; that we might be made the righteousness of God in him.

Philippians 3:9; And be found in him, not having mine own righteousness, which is of the law, but that which is through the faith of Christ, the righteousness which is of God by faith:

Romans 5:1; Therefore being justified by faith, we have peace with God through our Lord Jesus Christ:

Romans 8:1; There is therefore now no condemnation to them which are in Christ Jesus, who walk not after the flesh, but after the Spirit.

(e) *You Were Adopted*

You have a new identity as a child of God, joint heirs with Jesus.

John 1:12; But as many as received him, to them gave he power to become the sons of God, even to them that believe on his name:

Romans 8:15-17; 15 For ye have not received the spirit of bondage again to fear; but ye have received the Spirit of adoption, whereby we cry, Abba, Father. **16** The Spirit itself beareth witness with our spirit, that we are the children of God: **17** And if children, then heirs; heirs of God, and joint-heirs with Christ; if so be that we suffer with him, that we may be also glorified together.

Ephesians 2:19; Now therefore ye are no more strangers and foreigners, but fellowcitizens with the saints, and of the household of God;

IMPORTANT INFORMATION

(f) You Received Eternal Life

You have now received the life of God and a new nature. This is confirmed by a new and corresponding change in your actions.

Romans 6:23; For the wages of sin is death; but the gift of God is eternal life through Jesus Christ our Lord.

John 3:16; For God so loved the world, that he gave his only begotten Son, that whosoever believeth in him should not perish, but have everlasting life.

Ephesians 2:1-2; 1 And you hath he quickened, who were dead in trespasses and sins; 2 Wherein in time past ye walked according to the course of this world, according to the prince of the power of the air, the spirit that now worketh in the children of disobedience:

Ephesians 5:17; Wherefore be ye not unwise, but understanding what the will of the Lord is.

Ezekiel 36:26-27; A new heart also will I give you, and a new spirit will I put within you: and I will take away the stony heart out of your flesh, and I will give you an heart of flesh. 27 And I will put my spirit within you, and cause you to walk in my statutes, and ye shall keep my judgments, and do them.

1John 5:12-13; He that hath the Son hath life; and he that hath not the Son of God hath not life. 13 These things have I written unto you that believe on the name of the Son of God; that ye may know that ye have eternal life, and that ye may believe on the name of the Son of God.

---

3. The New Life in Christ and your Responsibilities

When you received Christ, you started a NEW life, which is holy and Godly. You must now live responsibly, be keenly aware of your actions, and demonstrate love towards others.

> **2Corinthians 5:17**; Therefore if any man be in Christ, he is a new creature: old things are passed away; behold, all things are become new.
>
> **Ephesians 2:4-5**; But God, who is rich in mercy, for his great love wherewith he loved us, **5** Even when we were dead in sins, hath quickened us together with Christ, (by grace ye are saved;)

(a) God has changed your nature (Regeneration)

> **Titus 3:5-6**; Not by works of righteousness which we have done, but according to his mercy he saved us, by the washing of regeneration, and renewing of the Holy Ghost; **6** Which he shed on us abundantly through Jesus Christ our Saviour;

Now you must *separate* yourself from the old life of sin and live a holy life. (e.g., living according to God's Word)

16

IMPORTANT INFORMATION

Romans 6:1-4; What shall we say then? Shall we continue in sin, that grace may abound? **2** God forbid. How shall we, that are dead to sin, live any longer therein? **3** Know ye not, that so many of us as were baptized into Jesus Christ were baptized into his death? **4** Therefore we are buried with him by baptism into death: that like as Christ was raised up from the dead by the glory of the Father, even so we also should walk in newness of life.

Galatians 5:19-24; Now the works of the flesh are manifest, which are these; Adultery, fornication, uncleanness, lasciviousness, **20** Idolatry, witchcraft, hatred, variance, emulations, wrath, strife, seditions, heresies, **21** Envyings, murders, drunkenness, revellings, and such like: of the which I tell you before, as I have also told you in time past, that they which do such things shall not inherit the kingdom of God. **22** But the fruit of the Spirit is love, joy, peace, longsuffering, gentleness, goodness, faith, **23** Meekness, temperance: against such there is no law. **24** And they that are Christ's have crucified the flesh with the affections and lusts.

Because some of your closest friends may be bad for you now, you must separate yourself from the influences and friendships that may lead you back into sin. Learn to be an example of holiness to your friends and demonstrate godly works. Get rid of signs of Satan's rule in your life. Where possible, correct all wrongs that you have done to others in the past.

Acts 19:18-20; And many that believed came, and confessed, and shewed their deeds. **19** Many of them also which used curious arts brought their books together, and burned them before all men: and they counted the price of them, and found it fifty thousand pieces of silver. **20** So mightily grew the word of God and prevailed.

17

IMPORTANT INFORMATION

Hebrews 12:14; Follow peace with all men, and holiness, without which no man shall see the Lord:

(b) *You must develop a personal relationship with God*

Learn to pray privately. Worship, consecration, confession of sin, supplication, intercession, spiritual warfare, and thanksgiving are all forms of prayer.

1Thessalonians 5:17; Pray without ceasing.

Matthew 6:6-13; But thou, when thou prayest, enter into thy closet, and when thou hast shut thy door, pray to thy Father which is in secret; and thy Father which seeth in secret shall reward thee openly. **7** But when ye pray, use not vain repetitions, as the heathen do: for they think that they shall be heard for their much speaking. **8** Be not ye therefore like unto them: for your Father knoweth what things ye have need of, before ye ask him. **9** After this manner therefore pray ye: Our Father which art in heaven, Hallowed be thy name. **10** Thy kingdom come, Thy will be done in earth, as it is in heaven. **11** Give us this day our daily bread. **12** And forgive us our debts, as we forgive our debtors. **13** And lead us not into temptation, but deliver us from evil: For thine is the kingdom, and the power, and the glory, for ever. Amen.

Read and study God's Word.

2Timothy 3:15-17; And that from a child thou hast known the holy scriptures, which are able to make thee wise unto salvation through faith which is in Christ Jesus. **16** All scripture is given by inspiration of God, and is profitable for doctrine, for reproof, for correction, for instruction in righteousness: **17** That the man of God may be perfect, thoroughly furnished unto all good works.

18

IMPORTANT INFORMATION

Hebrews 4:12; For the word of God is quick, and powerful, and sharper than any twoedged sword, piercing even to the dividing asunder of soul and spirit, and of the joints and marrow, and is a discerner of the thoughts and intents of the heart.

2Timothy 2:15; Study to shew thyself approved unto God, a workman that needeth not to be ashamed, rightly dividing the word of truth.

Psalm 119:7; I will praise thee with uprightness of heart, when I shall have learned thy righteous judgments.

(c)   Attend Church

Become part of all activities of God's people.

Hebrews 10:25; Not forsaking the assembling of ourselves together, as the manner of some is; but exhorting one another: and so much the more, as ye see the day approaching.

Psalm 84:10;   For a day in thy courts is better than a thousand. I had rather be a doorkeeper in the house of my God, than to dwell in the tents of wickedness.

Ephesians 3:14-15;   For this cause I bow my knees unto the Father of our Lord Jesus Christ, 15 Of whom the whole family in heaven and earth is named,

1Peter 2:9; But ye are a chosen generation, a royal priesthood, an holy nation, a peculiar people; that ye should shew forth the praises of him who hath called you out of darkness into his marvellous light;

(d) Be baptised in water.

Matthew 28:18-20; And Jesus came and spake unto them, saying, All power is given unto me in heaven and in earth. **19** Go ye therefore, and teach all nations, baptizing them in the name of the Father, and of the Son, and of the Holy Ghost: **20** Teaching them to observe all things whatsoever I have commanded you: and, lo, I am with you always, even unto the end of the world. Amen.

(e)   *Tell others about Jesus and the salvation we have in Him*

Witness the power of His salvation to others.

Luke 24:46-48;   And said unto them, Thus it is written, and thus it behooved Christ to suffer, and to rise from the dead the third day: **47** And that repentance and remission of sins should be preached in his name among all nations, beginning at Jerusalem. **48** And ye are witnesses of these things.

Daniel 12:3;   And they that be wise shall shine as the brightness of the firmament; and they that turn many to righteousness as the stars for ever and ever.

Proverbs 11:30; The fruit of the righteous is a tree of life; and he that winneth souls is wise.

(f)   *Begin To Serve God With Your Substance.*

Participate in tithes and offerings, promote the move of God, and help those in need.

Malachi 3:8-10; Will a man rob God?   Yet ye have robbed me.   But ye say, Wherein have we robbed thee?   In tithes and offerings. **9** Ye are cursed with a curse: for ye have robbed me, even this whole nation. **10** Bring ye all the tithes into the storehouse, that there may be meat in mine house, and prove me now herewith, saith the LORD of hosts, if I will not open you the windows of heaven, and pour you out a blessing, that there shall not be room enough to receive it.

Proverbs 3:9-10; Honour the LORD with thy substance, and with the firstfruits of all thine increase: **10** So shall thy barns be filled with plenty, and thy presses shall burst out with new wine.

4. Study Suggestions

Most teachers recommend starting the study by completing the entire Gospel of John. Afterwards, you may begin to read from the book of Genesis to Revelation. Pray before you read. Then, read and meditate on each verse and chapter. Try to read a minimum of one chapter a day (at least 15 verses).

Each day, try to answer the following question.

What did I learn?
1. About God, the Father, the Son and the Holy Ghost
2. About whom you are in Christ
3. About God's promises and you
4. About God's Commands - Is there a command you can obey or something that you must change?
5. What do I remember? You must practice the Word as you study it. Try to remember each scripture and try to find it again in the bible.

5. Holy Ghost Baptism and the New Life in the Spirit

Our God is a **Trinity** - One God in Three persons – The Father, the Son, and the Holy Ghost.

> **Matthew 3:16-17**; And Jesus, when he was baptized, went up straightway out of the water: and, lo, the heavens were opened unto him, and he saw the Spirit of God descending like a dove, and lighting upon him: **17** And lo a voice from heaven, saying, This is my beloved Son, in whom I am well pleased.

> **2Corinthians 13:14**; The grace of the Lord Jesus Christ, and the love of God, and the communion of the Holy Ghost, be with you all. Amen.

You belong to the Father, the Son died for you and the Holy Spirit works in your life of salvation. God wants to fill you with the Holy Ghost. He will give you the power to live right and to serve God in the beauty of holiness.

> **Titus 3:5;** Not by works of righteousness which we have done, but according to his mercy he saved us, by the washing of regeneration, and renewing of the Holy Ghost;

> **Acts 1:8;** But ye shall receive power, after that the Holy Ghost is come upon you: and ye shall be witnesses unto me both in Jerusalem, and in all Judaea, and in Samaria, and unto the uttermost part of the earth.

IMPORTANT INFORMATION

Romans 8:26-27; Likewise the Spirit also helpeth our infirmities: for we know not what we should pray for as we ought: but the Spirit itself maketh intercession for us with groanings which cannot be uttered. **27** And he that searcheth the hearts knoweth what is the mind of the Spirit, because he maketh intercession for the saints according to the will of God.

Acts 2:1-4; And when the day of Pentecost was fully come, they were all with one accord in one place. **2** And suddenly there came a sound from heaven as of a rushing mighty wind, and it filled all the house where they were sitting. **3** And there appeared unto them cloven tongues like as of fire, and it sat upon each of them. **4** And they were all filled with the Holy Ghost, and began to speak with other tongues, as the Spirit gave them utterance.

John 14:15-18; 23; If ye love me, keep my commandments. **16** And I will pray the Father, and he shall give you another Comforter, that he may abide with you for ever; **17** Even the Spirit of truth; whom the world cannot receive, because it seeth him not, neither knoweth him: but ye know him; for he dwelleth with you, and shall be in you. **18** I will not leave you comfortless: I will come to you. **23** Jesus answered and said unto him, If a man love me, he will keep my words: and my Father will love him, and we will come unto him, and make our abode with him.

John 16:7-14; Nevertheless I tell you the truth; It is expedient for you that I go away: for if I go not away, the Comforter will not come unto you; but if I depart, I will send him unto you. **8** And when he is come, he will reprove the world of sin, and of righteousness, and of judgment: **9** Of sin, because they believe not on me; **10** Of righteousness, because I go to my Father, and ye see me no more; **11** Of judgment, because the prince of this world is judged. **12** I have yet many things to say unto you, but ye cannot bear them now. **13** Howbeit when he, the Spirit of truth, is come, he will guide you into all truth: for he shall not speak of himself; but whatsoever he shall hear, that shall he speak: and he will shew you things to come. **14** He shall glorify me: for he shall receive of mine, and shall shew it unto you.

23

1Corinthians 14:2-5; For he that speaketh in an unknown tongue speaketh not unto men, but unto God: for no man understandeth him; howbeit in the spirit he speaketh mysteries. **3** But he that prophesieth speaketh unto men to edification, and exhortation, and comfort. **4** He that speaketh in an unknown tongue edifieth himself; but he that prophesieth edifieth the church. **5** I would that ye all spake with tongues but rather that ye prophesied: for greater is he that prophesieth than he that speaketh with tongues, except he interpret, that the church may receive edifying.

Jude 20; But ye, beloved, building up yourselves on your most holy faith, praying in the Holy Ghost,

Acts 2:38-39; Then Peter said unto them, Repent, and be baptized every one of you in the name of Jesus Christ for the remission of sins, and ye shall receive the gift of the Holy Ghost. **39** For the promise is unto you, and to your children, and to all that are afar off, even as many as the LORD our God shall call.

Luke 11:9-13; And I say unto you, Ask, it shall be given you; seek, and ye shall find; knock, and it shall be opened unto you. **10** For every one that asketh receiveth; and he that seeketh findeth; and to him that knocketh it shall be opened. **11** If a son shall ask bread of any of you that is a father, will he give him a stone? or if he ask a fish, will he for a fish give him a serpent? **12** Or if he shall ask an egg, will he offer him a scorpion? **13** If ye then, being evil, know how to give good gifts unto your children: how much more shall your heavenly Father give the Holy Spirit to them that ask him?

How do you receive the Holy Spirit?

ASK!

Luke 11:13; If ye then, being evil, know how to give good gifts unto your children: how much more shall your heavenly Father give the Holy Spirit to them that ask him?

24

IMPORTANT INFORMATION

Believe and give thanks

> **Mark 11:24**; Therefore I say unto you, What things soever ye desire, when ye pray, believe that ye receive them, and ye shall have them.

Allow the Holy Ghost speak through you in other tongues as HE gives the utterance. Remember, this evidence must not be an act out of your desire to please those around you but you must wait allow it be a genuine move of God.

> **Acts 2:4**; And they were all filled with the Holy Ghost, and began to speak with other tongues, as the Spirit gave them utterance.

The Holy Spirit comes into your life as a Helper, Leader, and Friend. Live your life in communion (friendship), obedience (Leader) and dependence (helper) on the Holy Spirit.

> **Zechariah 4:6**; Then he answered and spake unto me, saying, This is the word of the LORD unto Zerubbabel, saying, Not by might, nor by power, but by my spirit, saith the LORD of hosts.
> **2Corinthians. 13:14**; The grace of the Lord Jesus Christ, and the love of God, and the communion of the Holy Ghost, be with you all. Amen.
> **Romans 8:14**; For as many as are led by the Spirit of God, they are the sons of God.

Let the character of the Holy Ghost guide your life, desires, and allow His gifts to reign in you. Let the fruit of the Spirit flow.

6. Serving and Worshipping God

Salvation brings you to your rightful place in god. You are now in a place to do exactly what you were created to do. This is your real purpose in life. Jesus saved you to allow you to become a true Worshipper of the Father.

> **John 4:23-24**; But the hour cometh, and now is, when the true worshippers shall worship the Father in spirit and in truth: for the Father seeketh such to worship him. **24** God is a Spirit: and they that worship him must worship him in spirit and in truth.

True salvation yields RIGHTEOUSNESS and PRAISE.

> **Isaiah 61:11**; For as the earth bringeth forth her bud, and as the garden causeth the things that are sown in it to spring forth; so the Lord GOD will cause righteousness and praise to spring forth before all the nations.

Worship is individual and corporate.

> **Psalm 108:3-5**;   I will praise thee, O LORD, among the people: and I will sing praises unto thee among the nations. **4** For thy mercy is great above the heavens: and thy truth reacheth unto the clouds. **5** Be thou exalted, O God, above the heavens: and thy glory above all the earth;

> **Psalm 150**;   Praise ye the LORD. Praise God in his sanctuary: praise him in the firmament of his power. **2** Praise him for his mighty acts: praise him according to his excellent greatness. **3** Praise him with the sound of the trumpet: praise him with the psaltery and harp. **4** Praise him with the timbrel and dance: praise him with stringed instruments and organs. **5** Praise him upon the loud cymbals: praise him upon the high sounding

cymbals. **6** Let every thing that hath breath praise the LORD. Praise ye the LORD.

Acts 2:47; Praising God, and having favour with all the people. And the Lord added to the church daily such as should be saved.

Worship from the heart with your life, actions, and words (singing, speaking to God).

Ephesians 5:18-20; And be not drunk with wine, wherein is excess; but be filled with the Spirit; **19** Speaking to yourselves in psalms and hymns and spiritual songs, singing and making melody in your heart to the Lord; **20** Giving thanks always for all things unto God and the Father in the name of our Lord Jesus Christ;

Worship and sing in the Spirit.

1Corinthians 14:15; What is it then? I will pray with the spirit, and I will pray with the understanding also: I will sing with the spirit, and I will sing with the understanding also.

Worship is verbally acknowledging who God is to you. You are not like those in the latter part of the verses below.

Romans 1:19-21; Because that which may be known of God is manifest in them; for God hath shewed it unto them. **20** For the invisible things of him from the creation of the world are clearly seen, being understood by the things that are made, even his eternal power and Godhead; so that they are without excuse: **21** Because that, when they knew God, they glorified him not as God, neither were thankful; but became vain in their imaginations, and their foolish heart was darkened.

IMPORTANT INFORMATION

MEMORY VERSES:

Matthew 9:37-38;   Then saith he unto his disciples, The harvest truly is plenteous, but the labourers are few; **38** Pray ye therefore the Lord of the harvest, that he will send forth labourers into his harvest.

John 4:23-24; But the hour cometh, and now is, when the true worshippers shall worship the Father in spirit and in truth: for the Father seeketh such to worship him. **24** God is a Spirit: and they that worship him must worship him in spirit and in truth.

IMPORTANT INFORMATION

El-Shaddi – The All Sufficient One

The Seven Redemptive Names Of Jehovah		Satan's Destructive Symptoms
Jehovah Jireh	The Lord my **Provider**	Poverty, lack, shortage, want, need, emptiness
Jehovah Nissi	The Lord my **Victory**	Battles, wars, hindering spirits, obstacles to faith
Jehovah Raah	The Lord my **Shepherd**	Confusion, neglect, unsure of direction, not knowing which way to go
Jehovah Rapha:	The Lord my **Healer**	Disease, sickness, weakness, brokenness
Jehovah Shalom:	The Lord my **Peace**	Emotional instability, fear, anxiety, insecurity
Jehovah Shammah:	The Lord who is **Ever-present**	Feelings of being alone, forsaken, isolated, distanced, forgotten
Jehovah Tsidkenu	The Lord my **Righteousness**	Unrighteousness, sin, inequities, not upholding God's Word as supreme

IMPORTANT INFORMATION

Hebrews 10:35 Cast not away therefore your confidence, which hath great recompence of reward. [36] For ye have need of patience, that, after ye have done the will of God, ye might receive the promise.

Visas *(Experiences in God)*

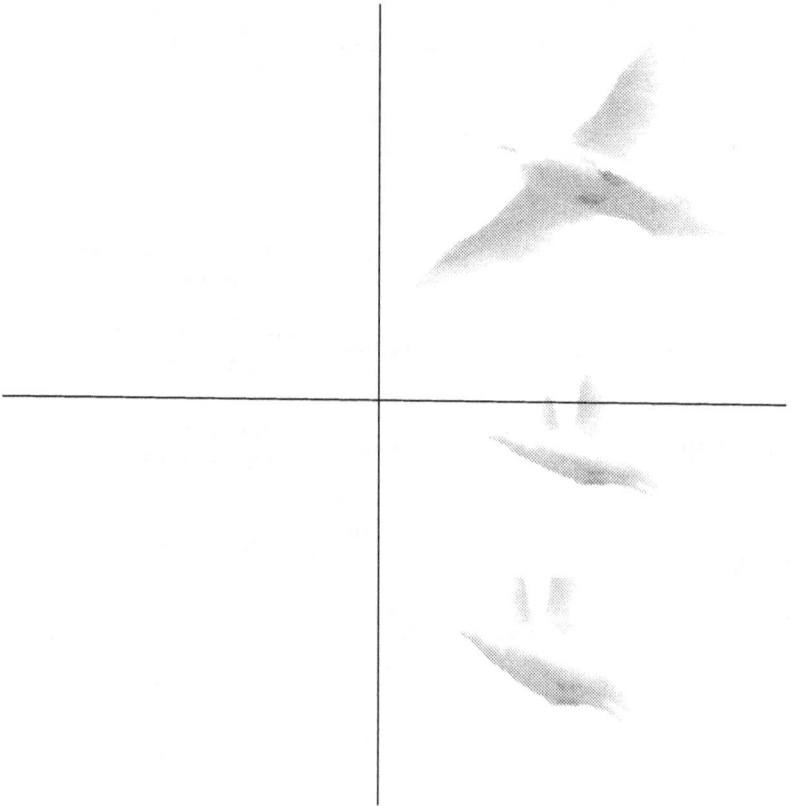

IMPORTANT INFORMATION

Ephesians 6:10 Finally, my brethren, be strong in the Lord, and in the power of His might. [11] Put on the whole armour of God, that ye may be able to stand against the wiles of the devil.

Visas *(Experiences in God)*

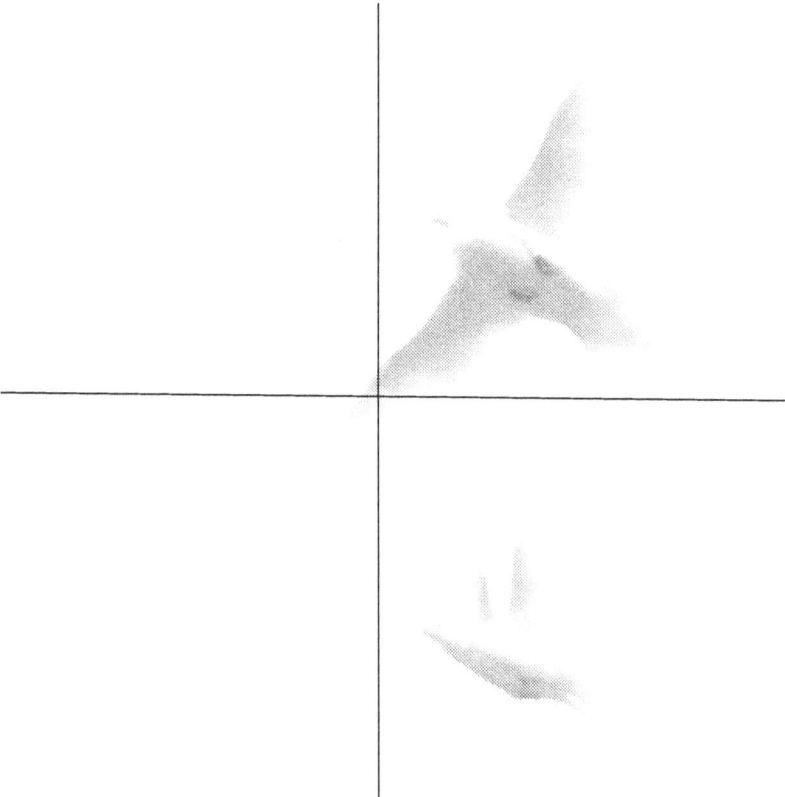

IMPORTANT INFORMATION

James 5:12 Confess your faults one to another, and pray one for another, that ye may be healed. The effectual fervent prayer of a righteous man availeth much.

Visas *(Experiences in God)*

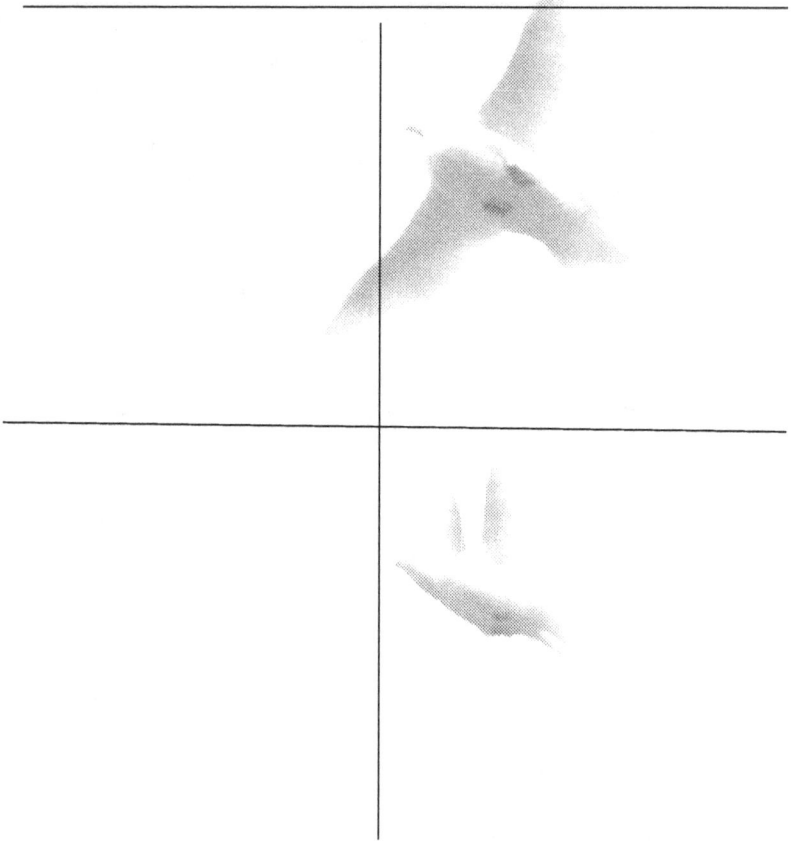

IMPORTANT INFORMATION

Genesis 32:28 And he said, Thy name shall be called no more Jacob, but Israel: for as a prince hast thou power with God and with men, and hast prevailed.

Visas *(Experiences in God)*

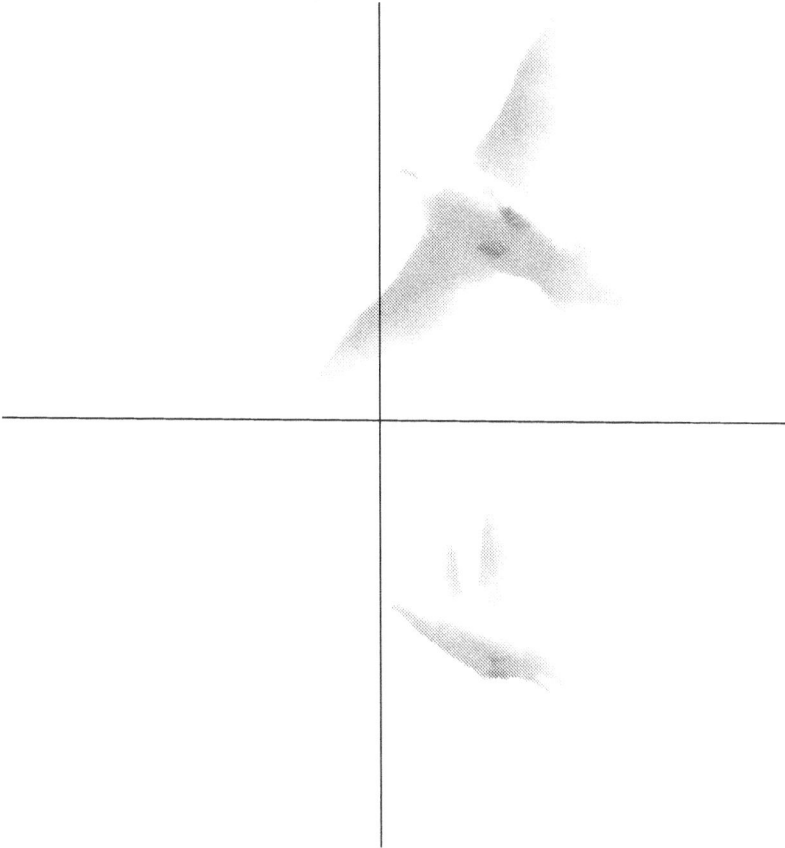

IMPORTANT INFORMATION

1 Kings 3:11 Behold, I have done according to thy words: lo, I have given thee a wise and an understanding heart; so that there was none like thee before thee, neither after thee shall any arise like unto thee.

Visas *(Experiences in God)*

IMPORTANT INFORMATION

Proverbs 3:7   Be not wise in thine own eyes: fear the LORD, and depart from evil.

Visas *(Experiences in God)*

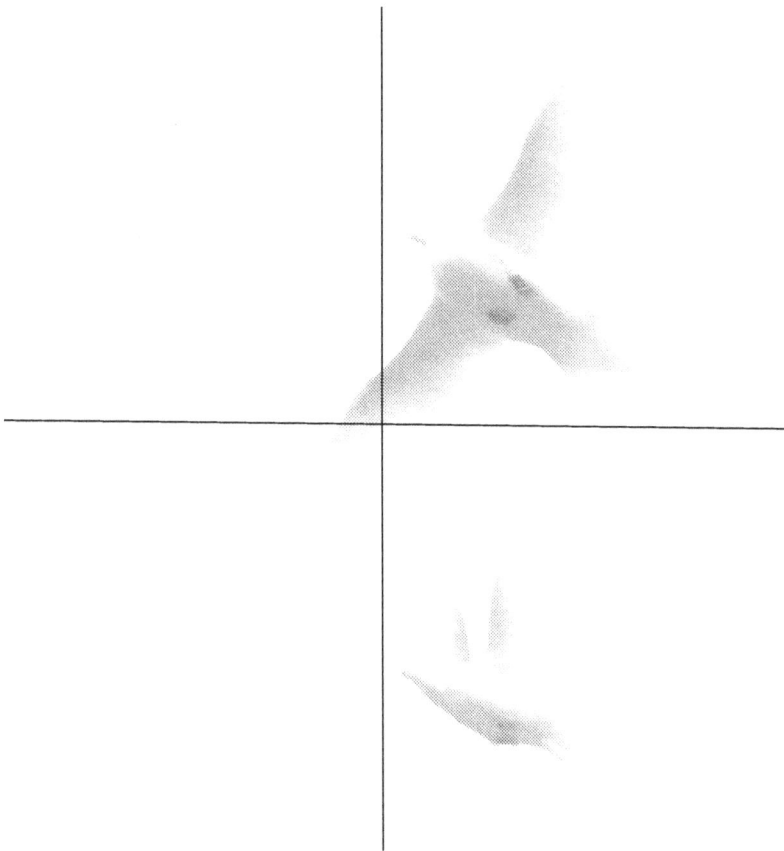

IMPORTANT INFORMATION

Proverbs 16:11 There is a way that seems right to a man, but in the end it leads to death.

Visas *(Experiences in God)*

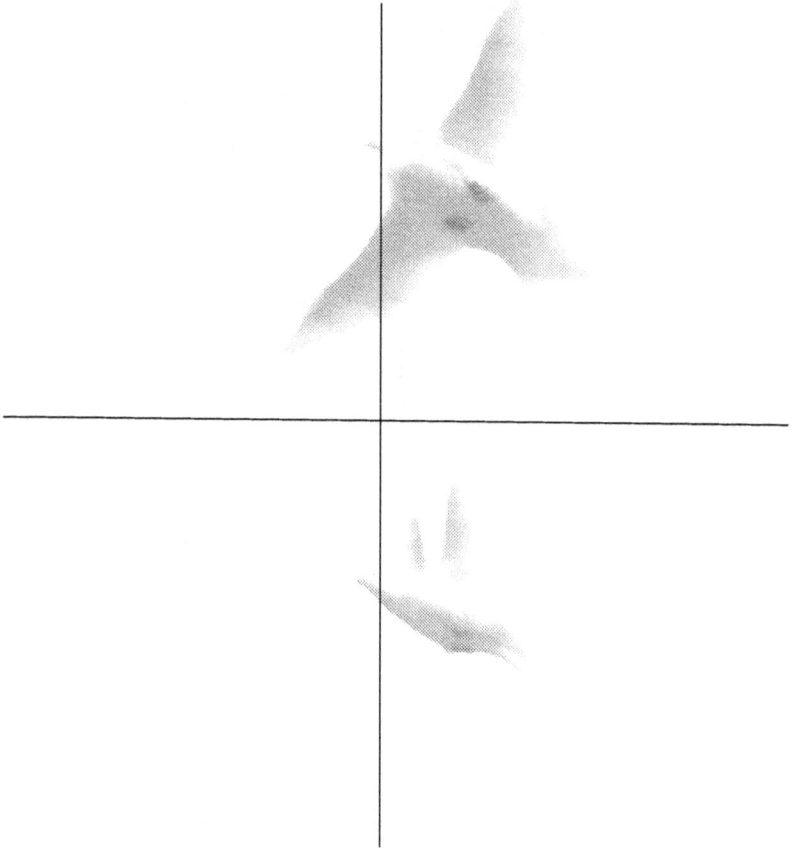

IMPORTANT INFORMATION

Proverbs 17:2 A wise servant shall have rule over a son that causeth shame, and shall have part of the inheritance among the brethren.

Visas *(Experiences in God)*

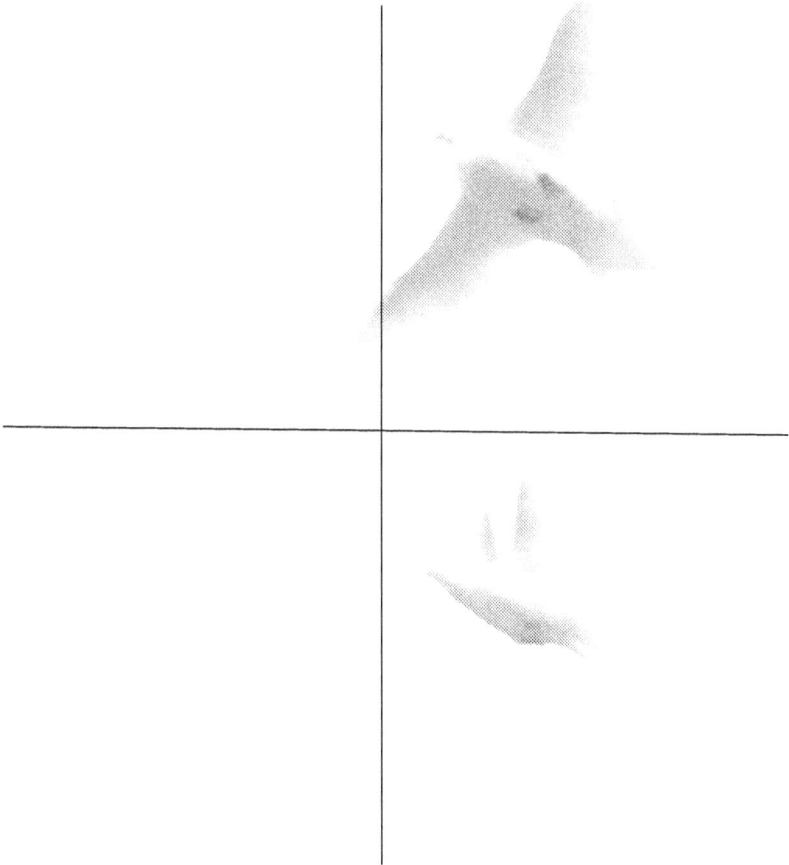

IMPORTANT INFORMATION

Proverbs 21:30 There is no wisdom nor understanding nor counsel against the LORD.

Visas *(Experiences in God)*

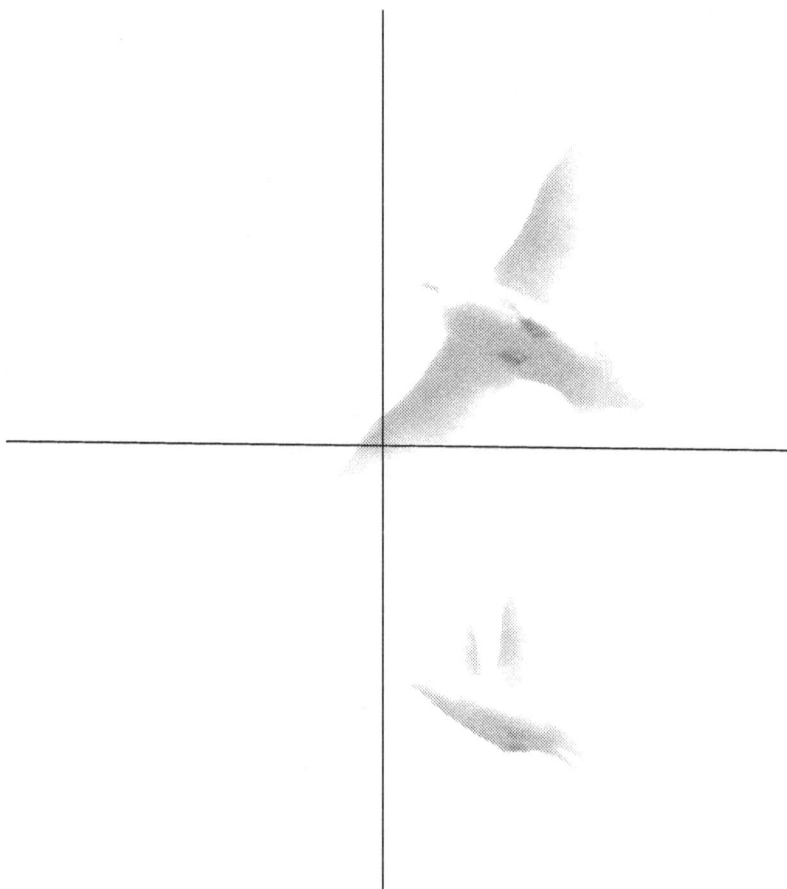

IMPORTANT INFORMATION

Luke 9:35 And there came a voice out of the cloud, saying, This is my beloved Son: hear him.

Visas *(Experiences in God)*

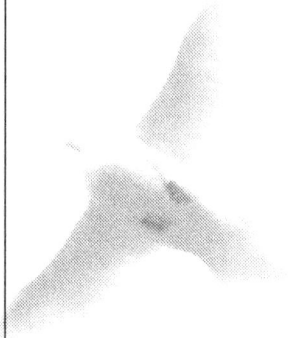

IMPORTANT INFORMATION

1 Corinthians 6:19 What? Know ye not that your body is the temple of the Holy Ghost which is in you, which ye have of God, and ye are not your own?

Visas *(Experiences in God)*

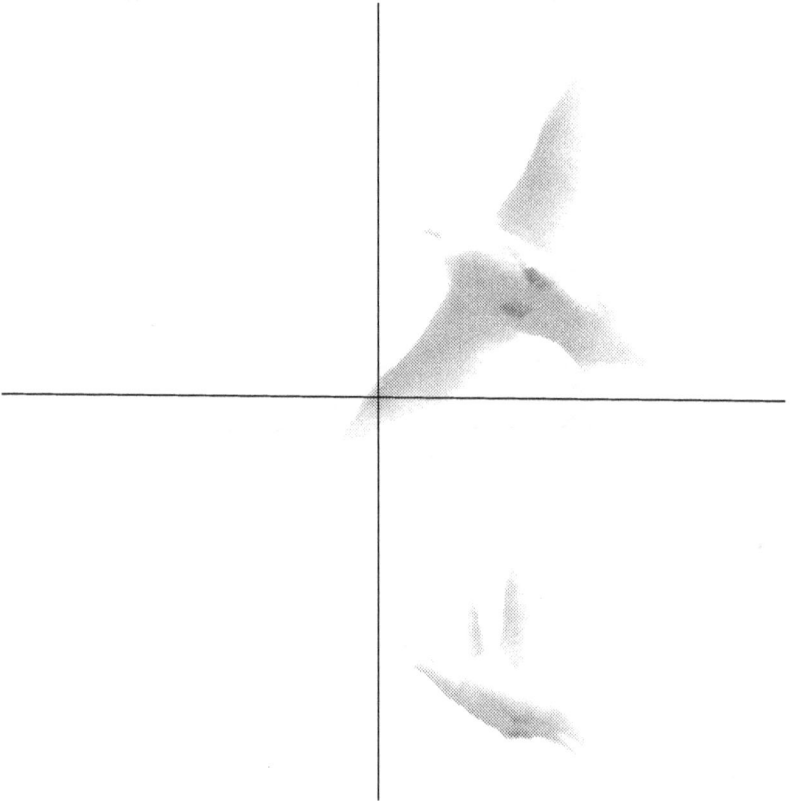

IMPORTANT INFORMATION

Joel 2:28 And it shall come to pass afterward, that I will pour out my spirit upon all flesh; and your sons and your daughters shall prophesy, your old men shall dream dreams, your young men shall see visions: (see also Acts 2:4)

Visas *(Experiences in God)*

IMPORTANT INFORMATION

Ezekiel 36:27 And I will put my spirit within you, and cause you to walk in my statutes, and ye shall keep my judgments, and do them.

Visas *(Experiences in God)*

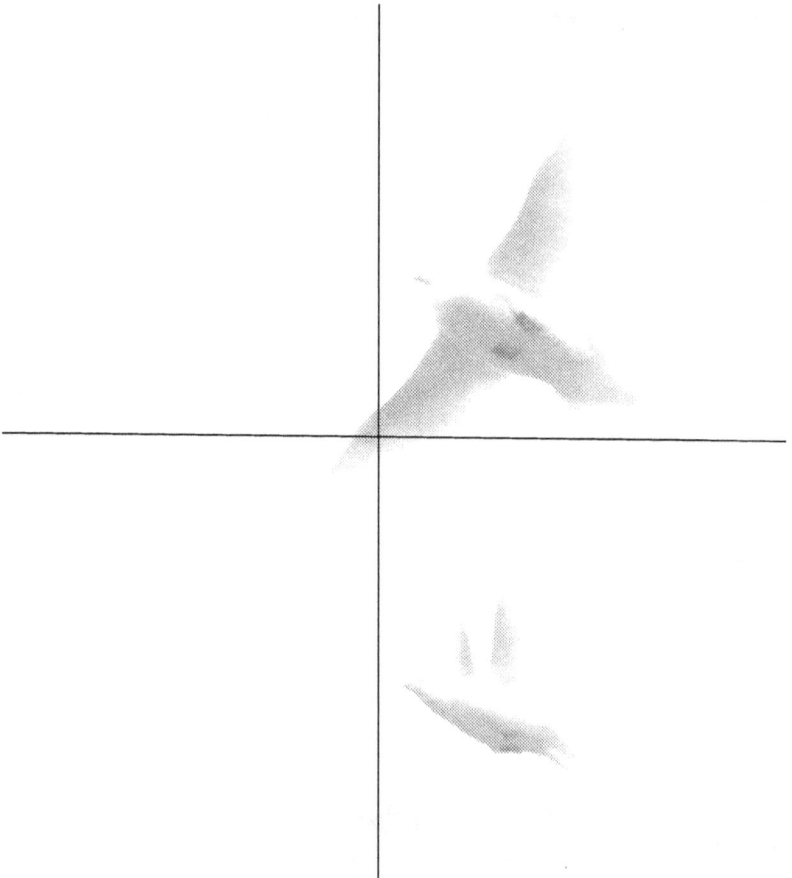

IMPORTANT INFORMATION

Luke 24:49 And, behold, I send the promise of my Father upon you: but tarry ye in the city of Jerusalem, until ye be endued with power from on high.

Visas *(Experiences in God)*

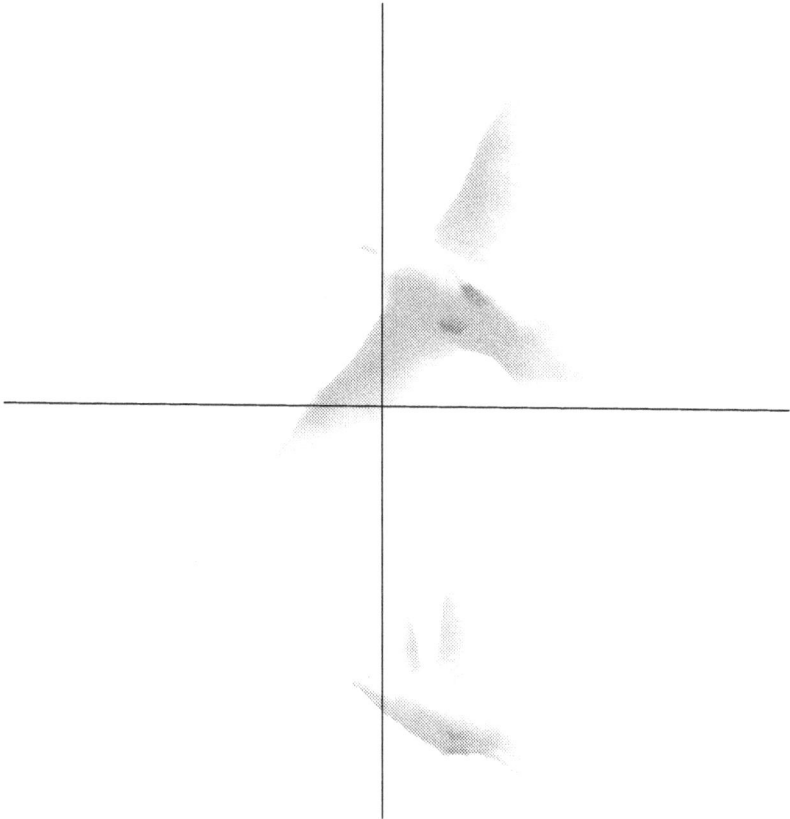

IMPORTANT INFORMATION

Acts 1:8 But ye shall receive power, after that the Holy Ghost is come upon you: and ye shall be witnesses unto me both in Jerusalem, and in all Judaea, and in Samaria, and unto the uttermost part of the earth.

Visas *(Experiences in God)*

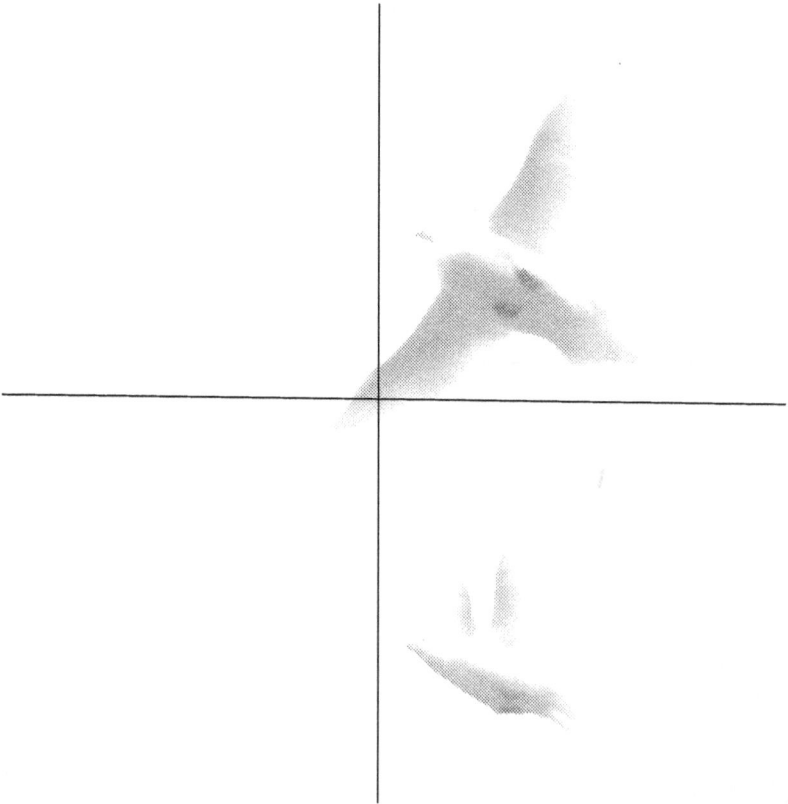

IMPORTANT INFORMATION

John 15:26 But when the Comforter is come, whom I will send unto you from the Father, even the Spirit of truth, which proceedeth from the Father, he shall testify of me:

Visas *(Experiences in God)*

IMPORTANT INFORMATION

John 14:26 But the Comforter, which is the Holy Ghost, whom the Father will send in my name, he shall teach you all things, and bring all things to your remembrance, whatsoever I have said unto you.

Visas *(Experiences in God)*

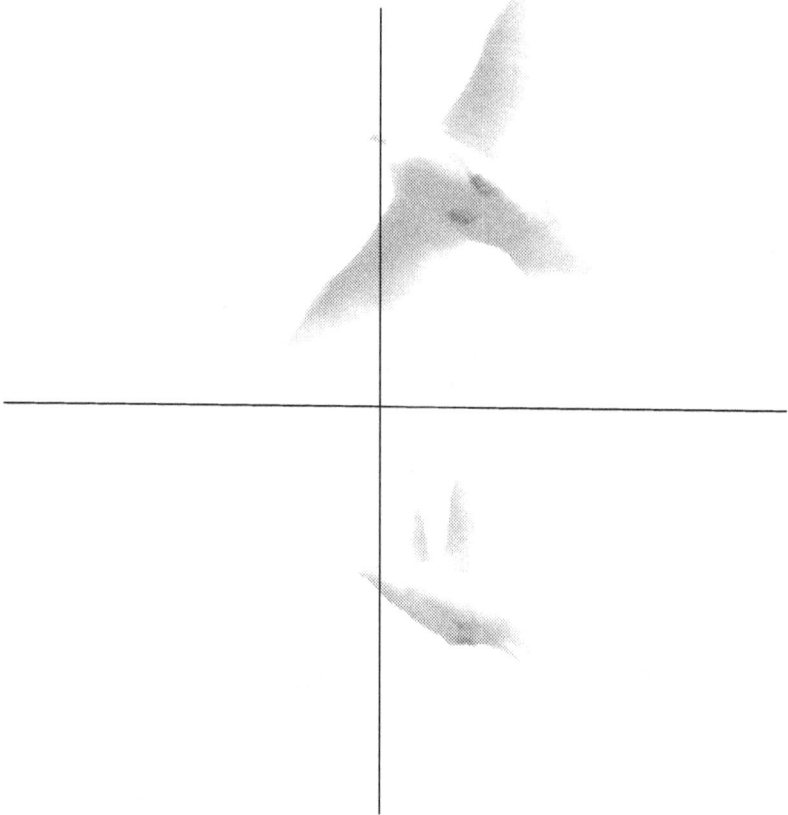

IMPORTANT INFORMATION

John 16:13 Howbeit when he, the Spirit of truth, is come, he will guide you into all truth: for he shall not speak of himself; but whatsoever he shall hear, that shall he speak: and he will shew you things to come.

Visas *(Experiences in God)*

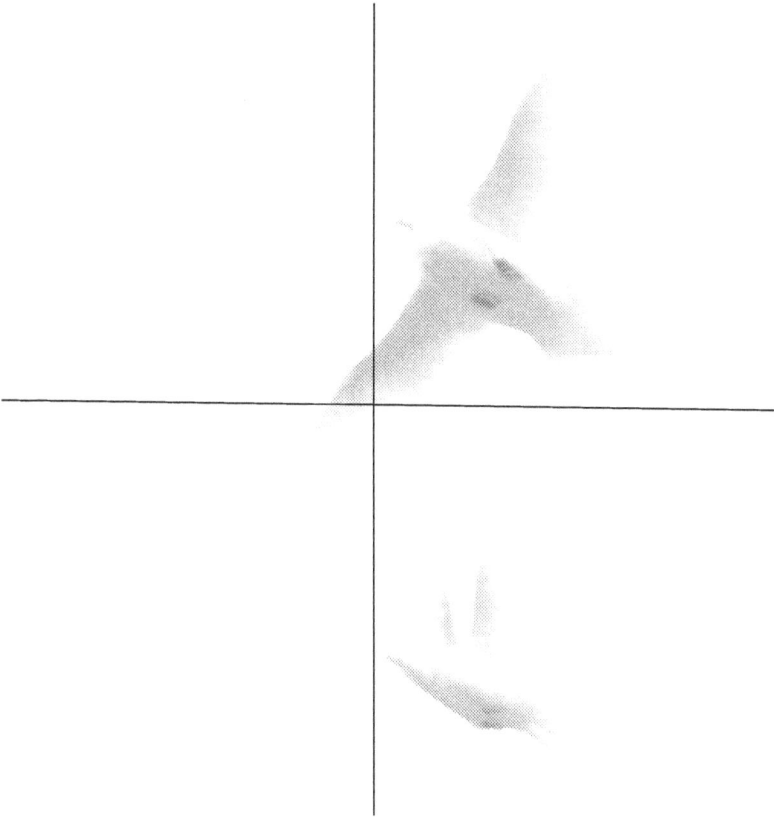

IMPORTANT INFORMATION

Acts 16:6 Now when they had gone throughout Phrygia and the region of Galatia, and were forbidden of the Holy Ghost to preach the word in Asia,

Visas *(Experiences in God)*

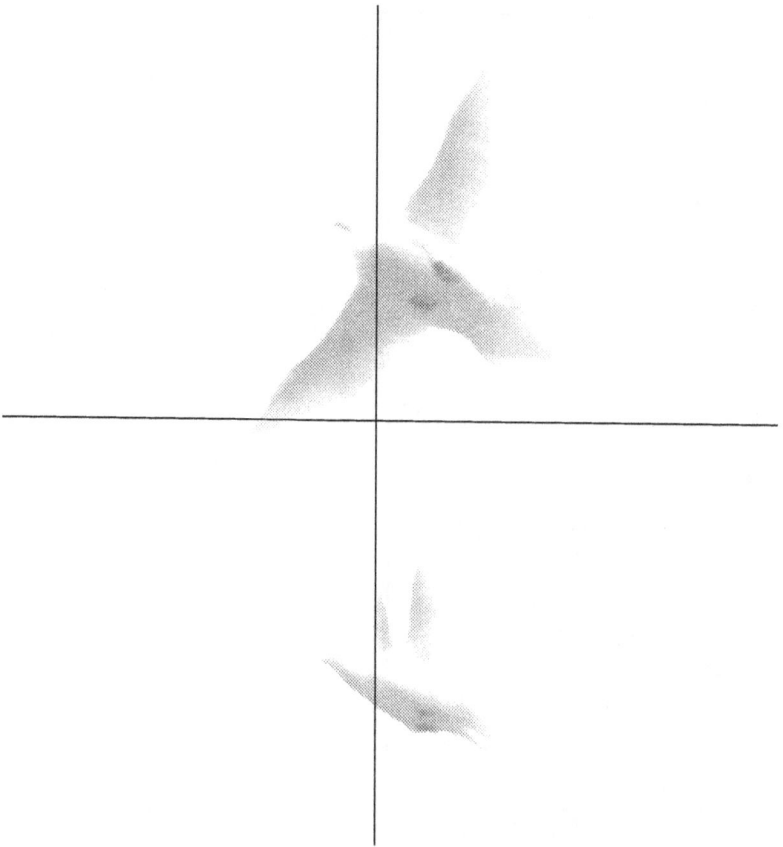

IMPORTANT INFORMATION

Romans 14:17 For the kingdom of God is not meat and drink; but righteousness, and peace, and joy in the Holy Ghost.

Visas *(Experiences in God)*

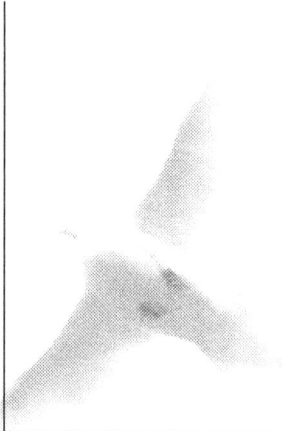

IMPORTANT INFORMATION

1Corinthians 4:20 For the kingdom of God is not in word, but in power.

Visas (Experiences in God)

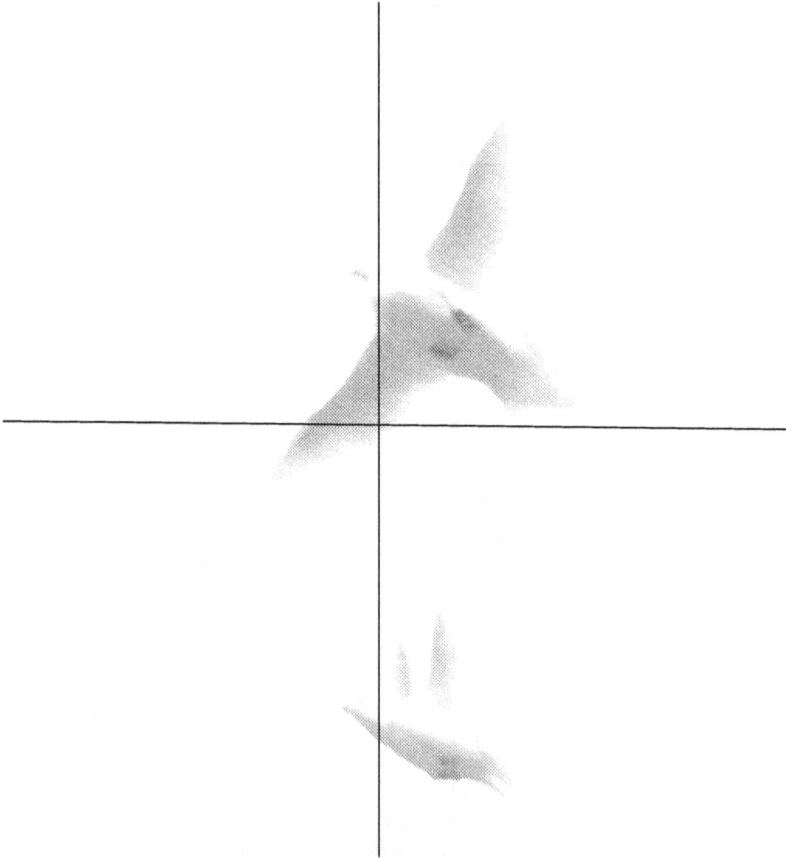

IMPORTANT INFORMATION

Luke 17:21 Neither shall they say, Lo here! or, lo there! for, behold, the kingdom of God is within you.

Visas *(Experiences in God)*

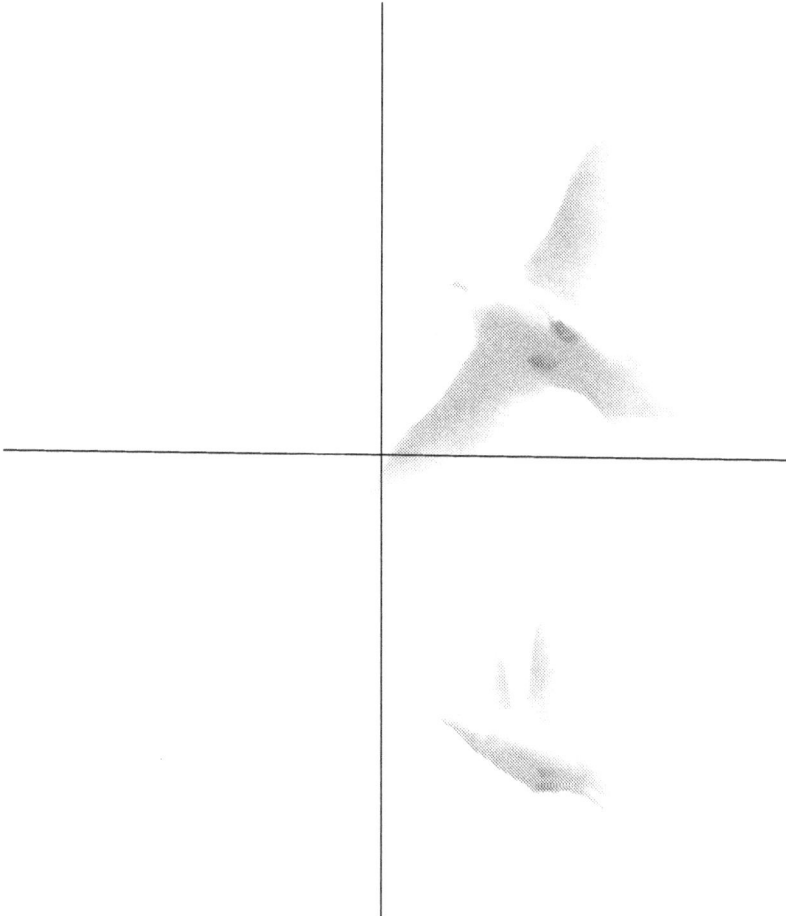

IMPORTANT INFORMATION

Ephesians 4:30 And grieve not the holy Spirit of God, whereby ye are sealed unto the day of redemption.

Visas *(Experiences in God)*

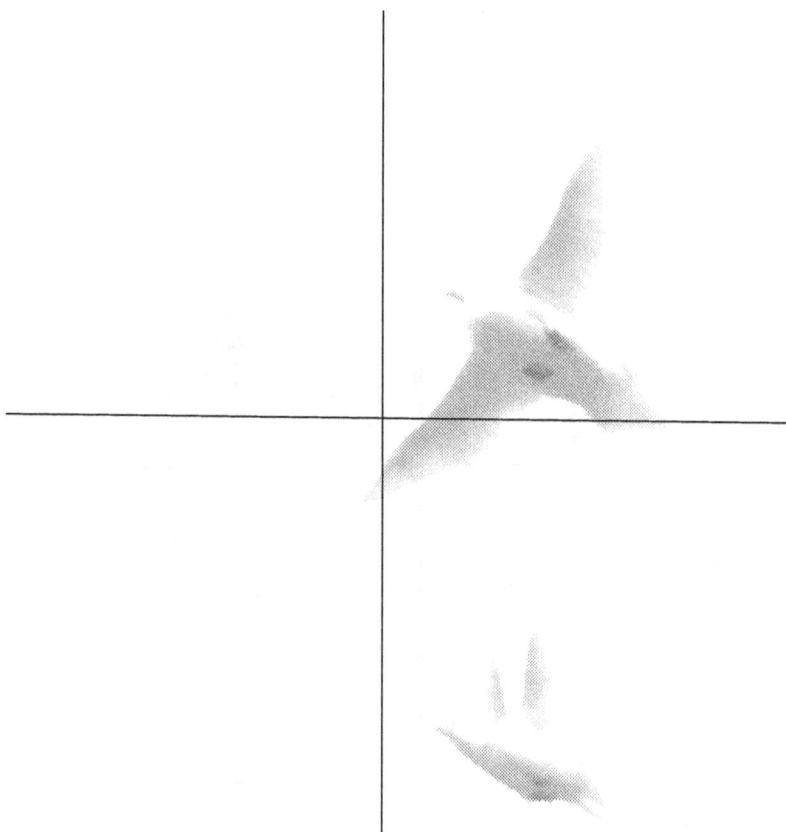

IMPORTANT INFORMATION

Romans 8:14 For as many as are led by the Spirit of God, they are the sons of God.

Visas *(Experiences in God)*

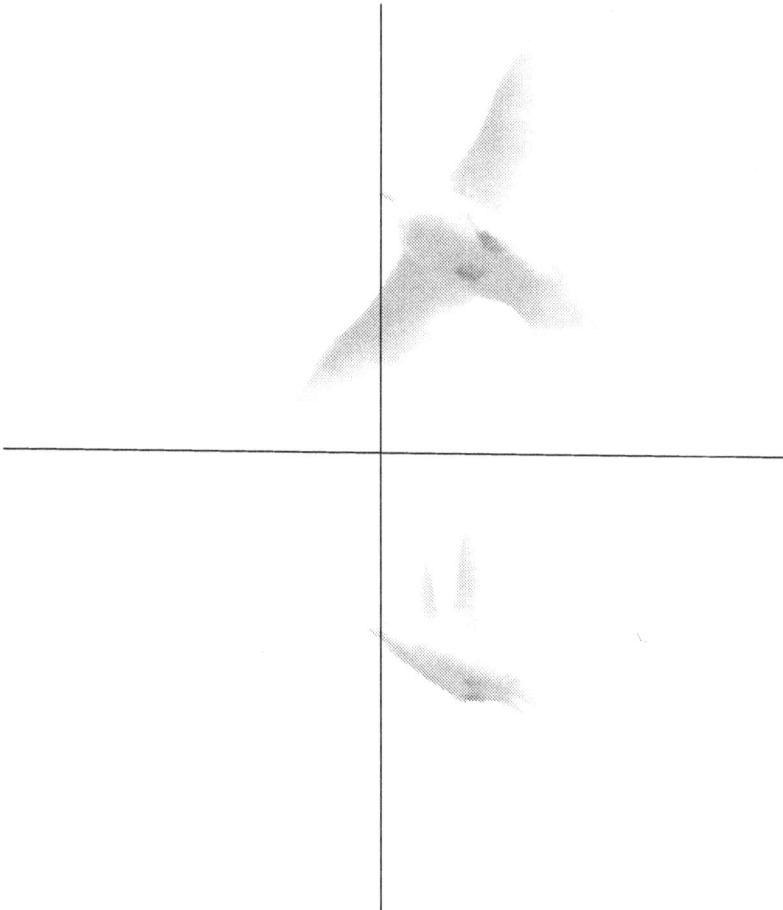

IMPORTANT INFORMATION

Titus 3:5 Not by works of righteousness which we have done, but according to his mercy he saved us, by the washing of regeneration, and renewing of the Holy Ghost;

Visas *(Experiences in God)*

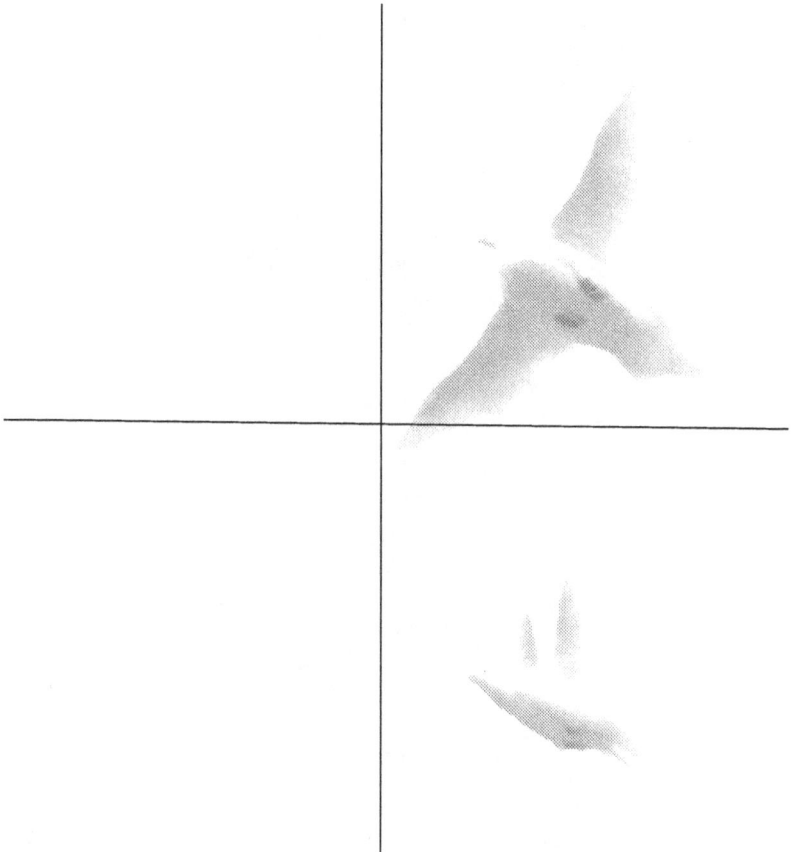

IMPORTANT INFORMATION

Isaiah 35:8 And an highway shall be there, and a way, and it shall be called The way of holiness; the unclean shall not pass over it; but it shall be for those: the wayfaring men, though fools, shall not err therein.

Visas *(Experiences in God)*

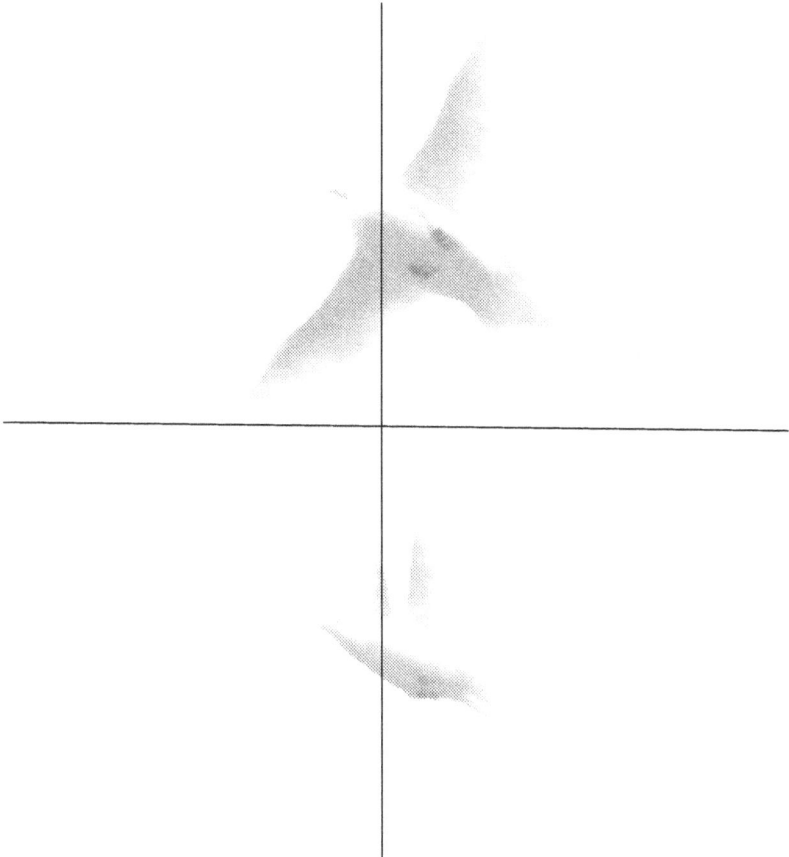

IMPORTANT INFORMATION

Psalms 14:1 The fool hath said in his heart, There is no God. They are corrupt, they have done abominable works, there is none that doeth good.

Visas *(Experiences in God)*

IMPORTANT INFORMATION

Proverbs 9:6 Forsake the foolish, and live; and go in the way of understanding.

Visas *(Experiences in God)*

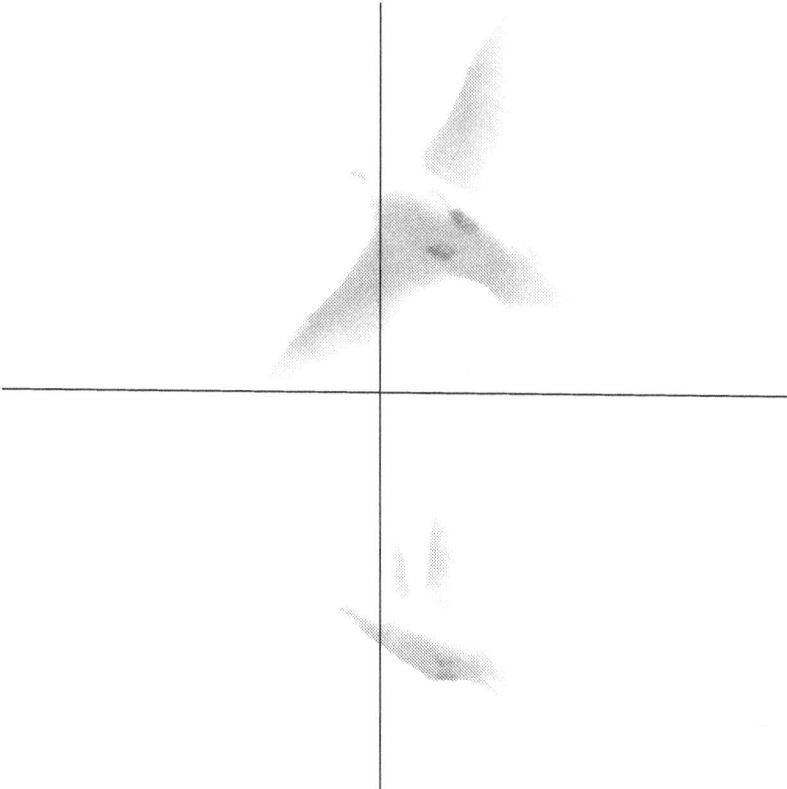

IMPORTANT INFORMATION

Matthew 8

12   And another of his disciples said unto him, **Lord, suffer me first to go and bury my father.**

Visas *(Experiences in God)*

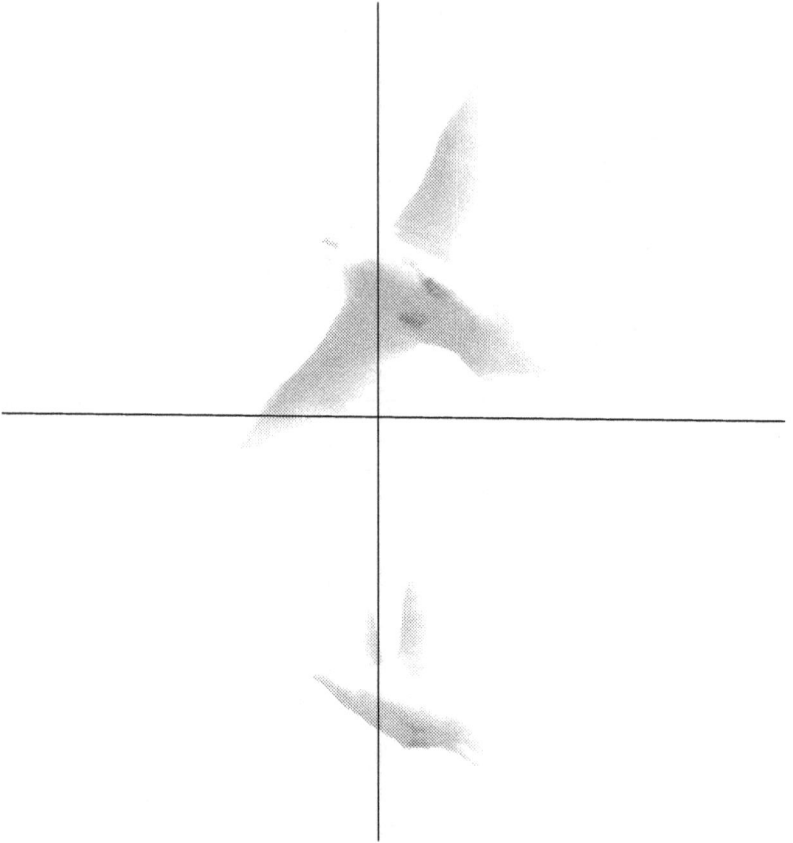

IMPORTANT INFORMATION

Romans 1:14 For the invisible things of him from the creation of the world are clearly seen, being understood by the things that are made, even his eternal power and Godhead; so that they are without excuse:

Visas *(Experiences in God)*

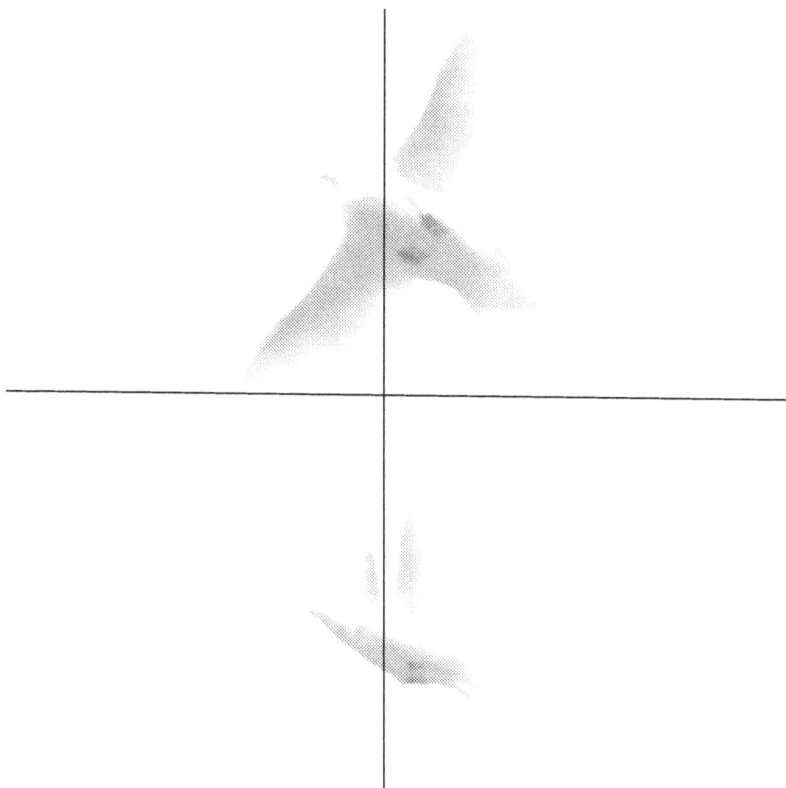

IMPORTANT INFORMATION

2 Timothy 2:15 Study to shew thyself approved unto God, a workman that needeth not to be ashamed, rightly dividing the word of truth.

Visas *(Experiences in God)*

IMPORTANT INFORMATION

---

1 Thessalonians 4:11 And that ye study to be quiet, and to do your own business, and to work with your own hands, as we commanded you;

Visas *(Experiences in God)*

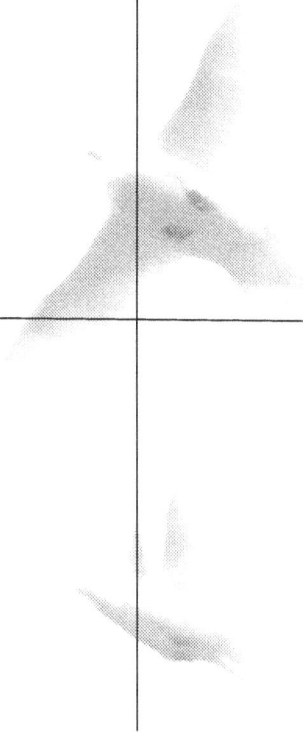

IMPORTANT INFORMATION

Proverbs 25:18 A man that beareth false witness against his neighbour is a maul, and a sword, and a sharp arrow.

Visas *(Experiences in God)*

IMPORTANT INFORMATION

Exodus 20:12 Honour thy father and thy mother: that thy days may be long upon the land which the LORD thy God giveth thee.

Visas *(Experiences in God)*

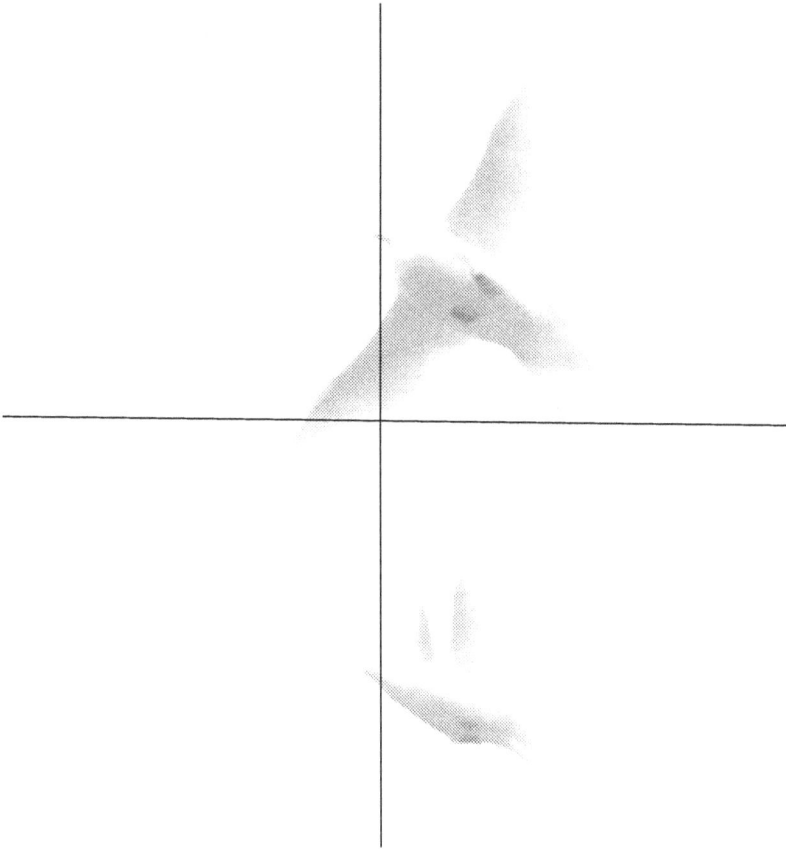

IMPORTANT INFORMATION

Proverbs 22:6 Train up a child in the way he should go: and when he is old, he will not depart from it.

Visas *(Experiences in God)*

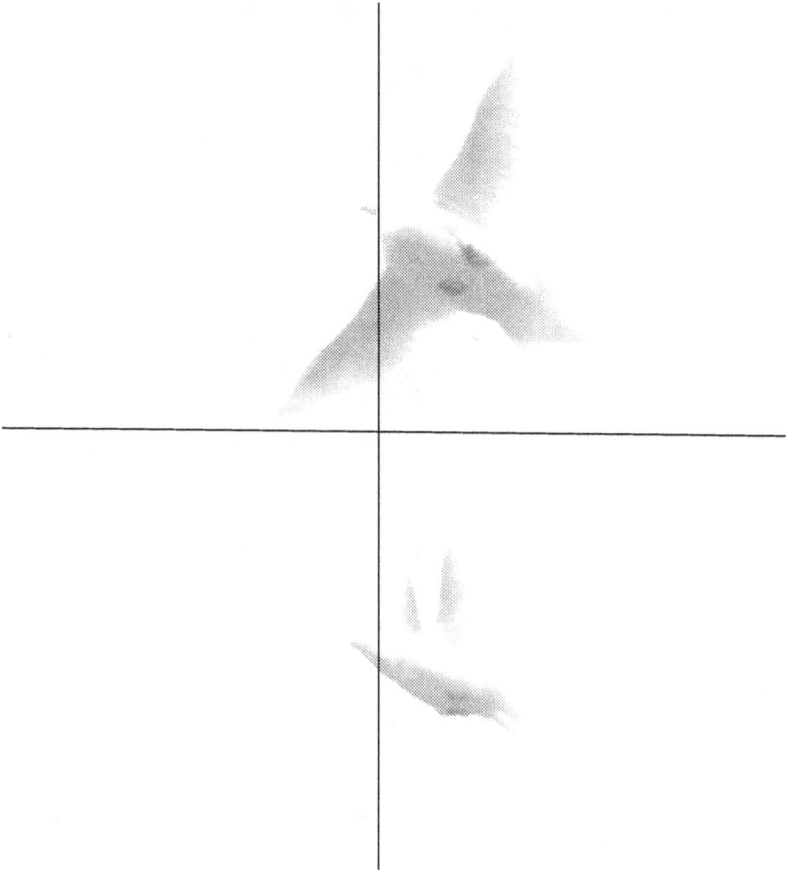

IMPORTANT INFORMATION

Proverbs 13:24 He that spareth his rod hateth his son: but he that loveth him chasteneth him betimes.

Visas *(Experiences in God)*

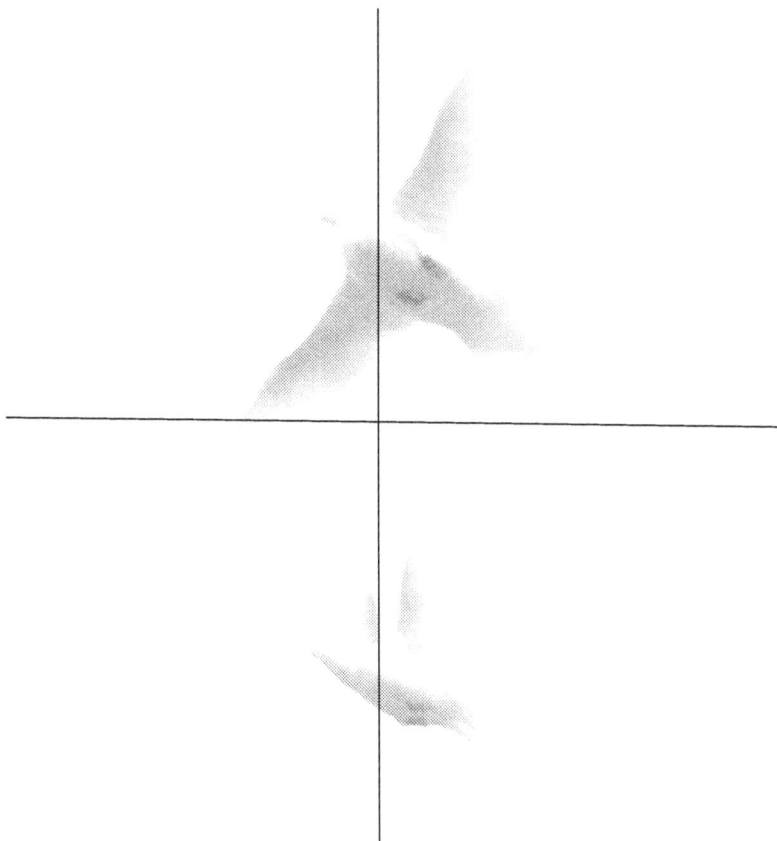

IMPORTANT INFORMATION

Matthew 10:41 He that receiveth a prophet in the name of a prophet shall receive a prophet's reward; and he that receiveth a righteous man in the name of a righteous man shall receive a righteous man's reward.

Visas *(Experiences in God)*

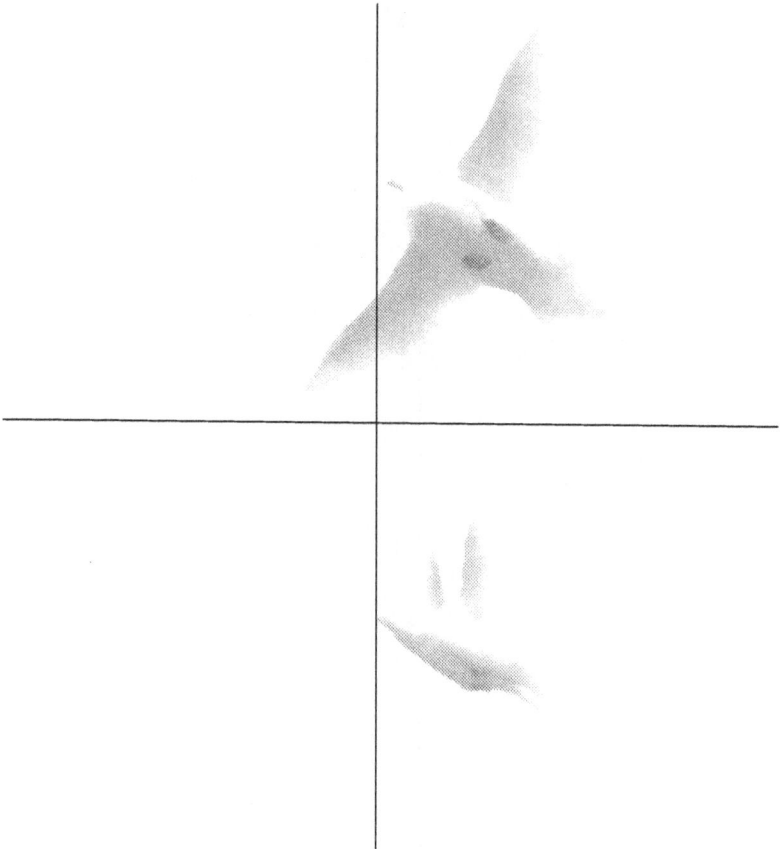

IMPORTANT INFORMATION

Hebrews 12:14 Follow peace with all men, and holiness, without which no man shall see the Lord:

Visas *(Experiences in God)*

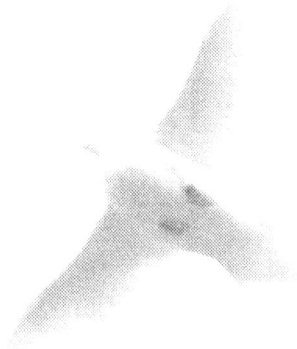

IMPORTANT INFORMATION

1 John 3:7 Little children, let no man deceive you: he that doeth righteousness is righteous, even as he is righteous.

Visas *(Experiences in God)*

IMPORTANT INFORMATION

Psalms 29:2 Give unto the LORD the glory due unto his name; worship the LORD in the beauty of holiness.

Visas *(Experiences in God)*

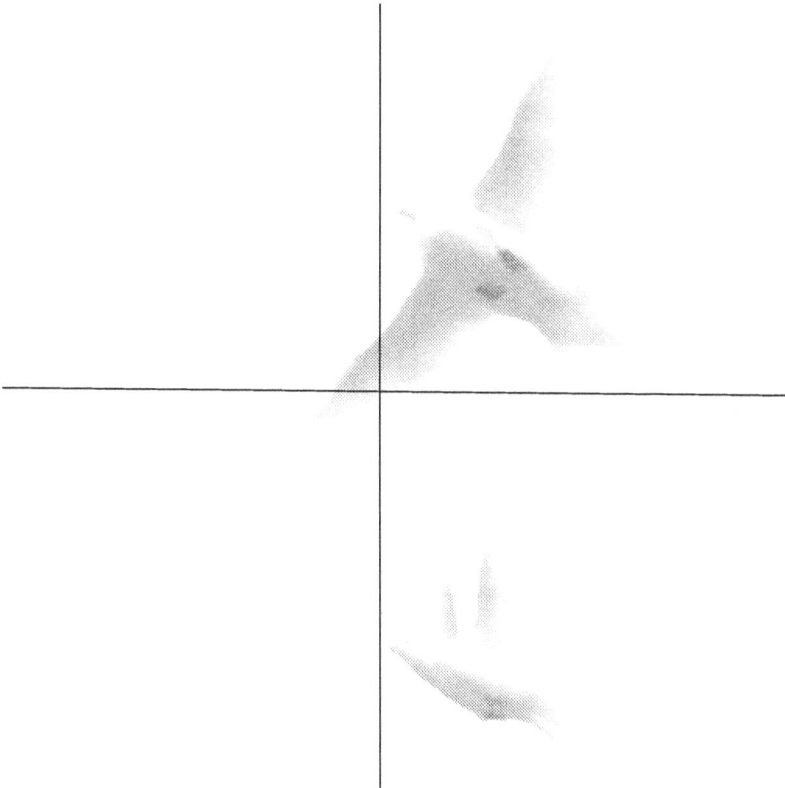

IMPORTANT INFORMATION

Proverbs 10:11 The mouth of a righteous man is a well of life: but violence covereth the mouth of the wicked.

Visas *(Experiences in God)*

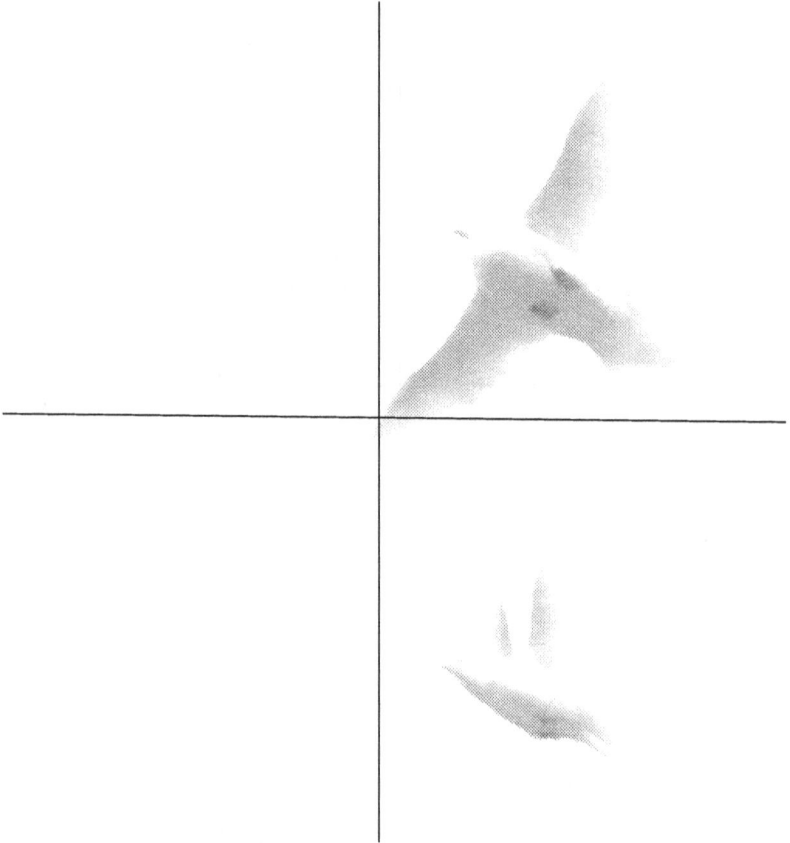

IMPORTANT INFORMATION

1Chronicles 16:29 Give unto the LORD the glory due unto his name: bring an offering, and come before him: worship the LORD in the beauty of holiness.

Visas *(Experiences in God)*

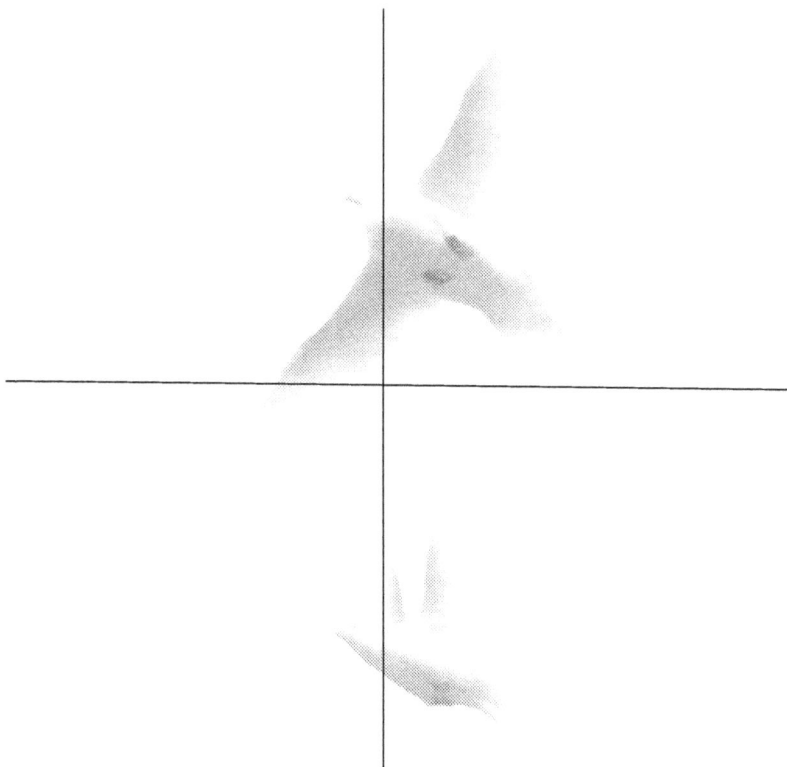

IMPORTANT INFORMATION

Ezekiel 18:4 Behold, all souls are mine; as the soul of the father, so also the soul of the son is mine: the soul that sinneth, it shall die.

Visas (Experiences in God)

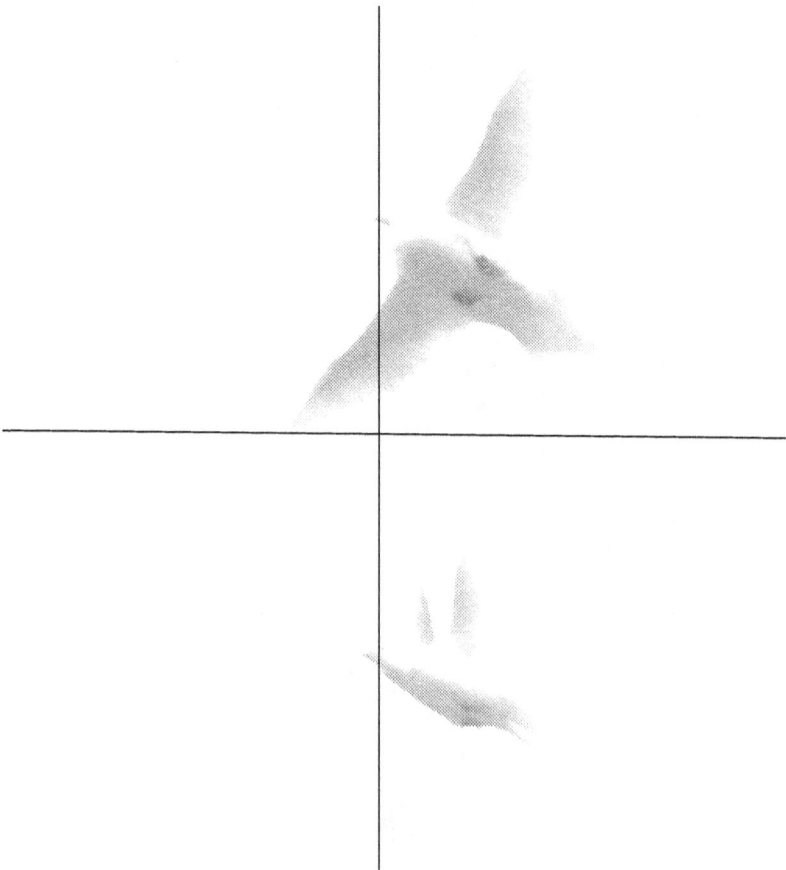

IMPORTANT INFORMATION

Genesis 1:26 And God said, Let us make man in our image, after our likeness: and let them have dominion over the fish of the sea, and over the fowl of the air, and over the cattle, and over all the earth, and over every creeping thing that creepeth upon the earth.

Visas *(Experiences in God)*

IMPORTANT INFORMATION

Psalms 8:6 Thou madest him to have dominion over the works of thy hands; thou hast put all things under his feet:

Visas *(Experiences in God)*

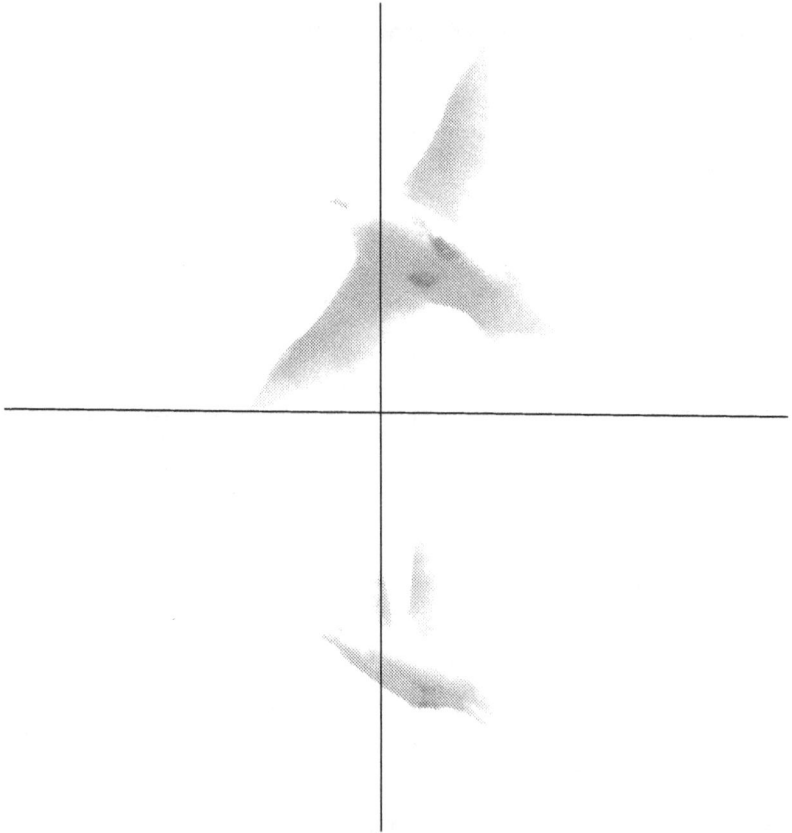

IMPORTANT INFORMATION

---

1 Corinthians 6:20 For ye are bought with a price: therefore glorify God in your body, and in your spirit, which are God's.

Visas *(Experiences in God)*

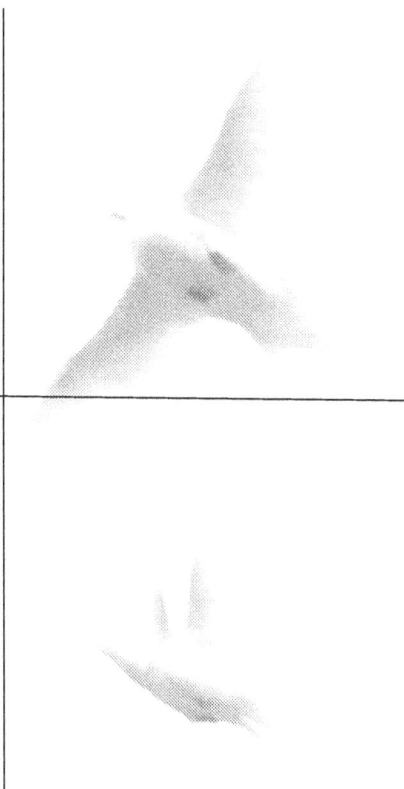

IMPORTANT INFORMATION

Quick Scriptural References		
Topic	**Passage**	**Text (King James Version)**
Why we need Salvation	**Romans. 3:23;**	For all have sinned, and come short of the glory of God;
	Romans. 6:23;	For the wages of sin is death; but the gift of God is eternal life through Jesus Christ our Lord.
	Romans. 5:12;	Wherefore, as by one man sin entered into the world, and death by sin; and so death passed upon all men, for that all have sinned:

IMPORTANT INFORMATION

Quick Scriptural References		
Topic	**Passage**	**Text (King James Version)**
What is the book of life?	Revelations.20:11-15	11 And I saw a great white throne, and him that sat on it, from whose face the earth and the heaven fled away; and there was found no place for them. 12 And I saw the dead, small and great, stand before God; and the books were opened: and another book was opened, which is the book of life: and the dead were judged out of those things which were written in the books, according to their works. 13 And the sea gave up the dead which were in it; and death and hell delivered up the dead which were in them: and they were judged every man according to their works. 14And death and hell were cast into the lake of fire. This is the second death. 15 And whosoever was not found written in the book of life was cast into the lake of fire.
Jesus; our only answer for sin	Romans 5:8;	But God commendeth his love toward us, in that, while we were yet sinners, Christ died for us.

Quick Scriptural References		
Topic	Passage	Text (King James Version)
Jesus; our only answer for sin	Isaiah 53:1-6;	1 Who hath believed our report? and to whom is the arm of the LORD revealed? 2 For he shall grow up before him as a tender plant, and as a root out of a dry ground: he hath no form nor comeliness; and when we shall see him, there is no beauty that we should desire him. 3 He is despised and rejected of men; a man of sorrows, and acquainted with grief: and we hid as it were our faces from him; he was despised, and we esteemed him not. 4 Surely he hath borne our griefs, and carried our sorrows: yet we did esteem him stricken, smitten of God, and afflicted. 5 But he was wounded for our transgressions, he was bruised for our iniquities: the chastisement of our peace was upon him; and with his stripes we are healed. 6 All we like sheep have gone astray; we have turned every one to his own way; and the LORD hath laid on him the iniquity of us all.

IMPORTANT INFORMATION

Quick Scriptural References		
Topic	**Passage**	**Text (King James Version)**
Jesus; our only answer for sin	John 14:6;	Jesus saith unto him, I am the way, the truth, and the life: no man cometh unto the Father, but by me.
	1 John 3:8;	He that committeth sin is of the devil; for the devil sinneth from the beginning. For this purpose the Son of God was manifested, that he might destroy the works of the devil.
	Acts 4:12	Neither is there salvation in any other: for there is none other name under heaven given among men, whereby we must be saved.
	John 3:16;	For God so loved the world, that he gave his only begotten Son, that whosoever believeth in him should not perish, but have everlasting life.
Repentance is necessary for salvation	2 Corinthians. 7:10;	For godly sorrow worketh repentance to salvation not to be repented of: but the sorrow of the world worketh death.

IMPORTANT INFORMATION

Quick Scriptural References		
Topic	**Passage**	**Text (King James Version)**
Repentance is necessary for salvation	**Romans 10:9-13;**	9 That if thou shalt confess with thy mouth the Lord Jesus, and shalt believe in thine heart that God hath raised him from the dead, thou shalt be saved. 10 For with the heart man believeth unto righteousness; and with the mouth confession is made unto salvation. 11 For the scripture saith, Whosoever believeth on him shall not be ashamed. 12 For there is no difference between the Jew and the Greek: for the same Lord over all is rich unto all that call upon him. 13 For whosoever shall call upon the name of the Lord shall be saved.
	Isaiah 55:6-7	6 Seek ye the LORD while he may be found, call ye upon him while he is near: 7 Let the wicked forsake his way, and the unrighteous man his thoughts: and let him return unto the LORD, and he will have mercy upon him; and to our God, for he will abundantly pardon.

IMPORTANT INFORMATION

Quick Scriptural References		
Topic	**Passage**	**Text (King James Version)**
By Grace and Faith in Jesus	**Ephesians 2:8-9;**	8 For by grace are ye saved through faith; and that not of yourselves: it is the gift of God: 9 Not of works, lest any man should boast.
Jesus – God's Son, brings salvation	**1John 5:11-13;**	11 And this is the record, that God hath given to us eternal life, and this life is in his Son. 12 He that hath the Son hath life; and he that hath not the Son of God hath not life. 13 These things have I written unto you that believe on the name of the Son of God; that ye may know that ye have eternal life, and that ye may believe on the name of the Son of God.
	John 6:37;	All that the Father giveth me shall come to me; and him that cometh to me I will in no wise cast out.
God promised salvation	**Titus 1:2;**	In hope of eternal life, which God, that cannot lie, promised before the world began;

IMPORTANT INFORMATION

Quick Scriptural References		
Topic	**Passage**	**Text (King James Version)**
You must be born again	**John 3:3;**	Jesus answered and said unto him, Verily, verily, I say unto thee, Except a man be born again, he cannot see the kingdom of God.
You must be born again	**1 Peter 1:23;**	Being born again, not of corruptible seed, but of incorruptible, by the word of God, which liveth and abideth for ever.
	Ephesians 2:1-2;	1 And you hath he quickened, who were dead in trespasses and sins; 2 Wherein in time past ye walked according to the course of this world, according to the prince of the power of the air, the spirit that now worketh in the children of disobedience:
Salvation makes us children of God	**John 1:12;**	But as many as received him, to them gave he power to become the sons of God, even to them that believe on his name:

IMPORTANT INFORMATION

Quick Scriptural References		
Topic	**Passage**	**Text (King James Version)**
	Romans 8:15-17;	15 For ye have not received the spirit of bondage again to fear; but ye have received the Spirit of adoption, whereby we cry, Abba, Father. 16 The Spirit itself beareth witness with our spirit, that we are the children of God: 17 And if children, then heirs; heirs of God, and joint-heirs with Christ; if so be that we suffer with him, that we may be also glorified together.
Joint Heirs with Christ	Ephesians. 2:19;	Now therefore ye are no more strangers and foreigners, but fellow citizens with the saints, and of the household of God;
All sin Forgiven	Isaiah 1:18;	Come now, and let us reason together, saith the LORD: though your sins be as scarlet, they shall be as white as snow; though they be red like crimson, they shall be as wool.
	Hebrews 8:12;	For I will be merciful to their unrighteousness, and their sins and their iniquities will I remember no more.
	1 John 1:9;	If we confess our sins, he is faithful and just to forgive us our sins, and to cleanse us from all unrighteousness.

Quick Scriptural References		
Topic	Passage	Text (King James Version)
On Righteousness	John 5:24;	Verily, verily, I say unto you, He that heareth my word, and believeth on him that sent me, hath everlasting life, and shall not come into condemnation; but is passed from death unto life.
	2 Corinthians 5:21;	For he hath made him to be sin for us, who knew no sin; that we might be made the righteousness of God in him.
	Philippians 3:9;	And be found in him, not having mine own righteousness, which is of the law, but that which is through the faith of Christ, the righteousness which is of God by faith:
On Faith	Romans 5:1;	Therefore being justified by faith, we have peace with God through our Lord Jesus Christ:
Walking with God	Romans 8:1;	There is therefore now no condemnation to them which are in Christ Jesus, who walk not after the flesh, but after the Spirit.
	Ephesians 5:17;	Wherefore be ye not unwise, but understanding what the will of the Lord is.

IMPORTANT INFORMATION

Quick Scriptural References		
Topic	**Passage**	**Text (King James Version)**
New Heart, and New Spirit	**Ezekiel 36:26-27;**	26 A new heart also will I give you, and a new spirit will I put within you: and I will take away the stony heart out of your flesh, and I will give you an heart of flesh. 27 And I will put my spirit within you, and cause you to walk in my statutes, and ye shall keep my judgments, and do them.
Paid by Jesus' Blood	**1 Peter 1:18-19;**	18 Forasmuch as ye know that ye were not redeemed with corruptible things, as silver and gold, from your vain conversation received by tradition from your fathers; 19 But with the precious blood of Christ, as of a lamb without blemish and without spot:

Quick Scriptural References		
Topic	**Passage**	**Text (King James Version)**
Faith brings salvation	Galatians 3:13-14;	13 Christ hath redeemed us from the curse of the law, being made a curse for us: for it is written, Cursed is every one that hangeth on a tree: 14 That the blessing of Abraham might come on the Gentiles through Jesus Christ; that we might receive the promise of the Spirit through faith.
Jesus Heals	1 Peter 2:24;	Who his own self bare our sins in his own body on the tree, that we, being dead to sins, should live unto righteousness: by whose stripes ye were healed.
God Riches	2 Cor.8:9;	For ye know the grace of our Lord Jesus Christ, that, though he was rich, yet for your sakes he became poor, that ye through his poverty might be rich.
Sins forgiven	Colossians 1:13-14;	13 Who hath delivered us from the power of darkness, and hath translated us into the kingdom of his dear Son: 14 In whom we have redemption through his blood, even the forgiveness of sins:

IMPORTANT INFORMATION

Quick Scriptural References		
Topic	**Passage**	**Text (King James Version)**
The new man	2 Corinthians 5:17;	Therefore if any man be in Christ, he is a new creature: old things are passed away; behold, all things are become new.
Saved by God	Ephesians 2:4-5;	4 But God, who is rich in mercy, for his great love wherewith he loved us, 5 Even when we were dead in sins, hath quickened us together with Christ, (by grace ye are saved;)
Prayer	1 Thessalonians 5:17;	Pray without ceasing.

Quick Scriptural References		
Topic	**Passage**	**Text (King James Version)**
How to pray	**Matthew 6:6-13;**	6 But thou, when thou prayest, enter into thy closet, and when thou hast shut thy door, pray to thy Father which is in secret; and thy Father which seeth in secret shall reward thee openly. 7 But when ye pray, use not vain repetitions, as the heathen do: for they think that they shall be heard for their much speaking. 8 Be not ye therefore like unto them: for your Father knoweth what things ye have need of, before ye ask him. 9 After this manner therefore pray ye: Our Father which art in heaven, Hallowed be thy name. 10 Thy kingdom come, Thy will be done in earth, as it is in heaven. 11 Give us this day our daily bread. 12 And forgive us our debts, as we forgive our debtors. 13 And lead us not into temptation, but deliver us from evil: For thine is the kingdom, and the power, and the glory, for ever. Amen.

IMPORTANT INFORMATION

Quick Scriptural References		
Topic	**Passage**	**Text (King James Version)**
Studying God's Word	**2 Timothy 3:15-17;**	15 And that from a child thou hast known the holy scriptures, which are able to make thee wise unto salvation through faith which is in Christ Jesus. 16 All scripture is given by inspiration of God, and is profitable for doctrine, for reproof, for correction, for instruction in righteousness: 17 That the man of God may be perfect, thoroughly furnished unto all good works.
	Hebrews 4:12;	For the word of God is quick, and powerful, and sharper than any twoedged sword, piercing even to the dividing asunder of soul and spirit, and of the joints and marrow, and is a discerner of the thoughts and intents of the heart.
	2 Timothy 2:15;	Study to shew thyself approved unto God, a workman that needeth not to be ashamed, rightly dividing the word of truth.
	Psalm 119:7;	I will praise thee with uprightness of heart, when I shall have learned thy righteous judgments.

Quick Scriptural References		
Topic	**Passage**	**Text (King James Version)**
The Church Assembly	Hebrews 10:25;	Not forsaking the assembling of ourselves together, as the manner of some is; but exhorting one another: and so much the more, as ye see the day approaching.
	Psalm 84:10;	For a day in thy courts is better than a thousand. I had rather be a doorkeeper in the house of my God, than to dwell in the tents of wickedness.
	Ephesians 3:14-15;	14 For this cause I bow my knees unto the Father of our Lord Jesus Christ, 15 Of whom the whole family in heaven and earth is named,
	1 Peter 2:9;	But ye are a chosen generation, a royal priesthood, an holy nation, a peculiar people; that ye should shew forth the praises of him who hath called you out of darkness into his marvellous light;

Quick Scriptural References		
Topic	Passage	Text (King James Version)
Holy Ghost Power	Matthew 28:18-20	18 And Jesus came and spake unto them, saying, All power is given unto me in heaven and in earth. 19 Go ye therefore, and teach all nations, baptizing them in the name of the Father, and of the Son, and of the Holy Ghost: 20 Teaching them to observe all things whatsoever I have commanded you: and, lo, I am with you always, even unto the end of the world. Amen.
Christ's Witnesses	Luke 24:46-48;	46 And said unto them, Thus it is written, and thus it behooved Christ to suffer, and to rise from the dead the third day: 47 And that repentance and remission of sins should be preached in his name among all nations, beginning at Jerusalem. 48 And ye are witnesses of these things.
	Daniel 12:3;	And they that be wise shall shine as the brightness of the firmament; and they that turn many to righteousness as the stars for ever and ever.

Quick Scriptural References		
Topic	**Passage**	**Text (King James Version)**
Christ's Witnesses	**Proverbs 11:30;**	The fruit of the righteous is a tree of life; and he that winneth souls is wise.
On Giving	**Malachi 3:8-10;**	8 Will a man rob God? Yet ye have robbed me. But ye say, Wherein have we robbed thee? In tithes and offerings. 9 Ye are cursed with a curse: for ye have robbed me, even this whole nation. 10 Bring ye all the tithes into the storehouse, that there may be meat in mine house, and prove me now herewith, saith the LORD of hosts, if I will not open you the windows of heaven, and pour you out a blessing, that there shall not be room enough to receive it.
	Proverbs 3:9-10;	9 Honour the LORD with thy substance, and with the firstfruits of all thine increase: 10 So shall thy barns be filled with plenty, and thy presses shall burst out with new wine.

IMPORTANT INFORMATION

Quick Scriptural References		
Topic	**Passage**	**Text (King James Version)**
The Trinity	Matthew 3:16-17;	16 And Jesus, when he was baptized, went up straightway out of the water: and, lo, the heavens were opened unto him, and he saw the Spirit of God descending like a dove, and lighting upon him: 17 And lo a voice from heaven, saying, This is my beloved Son, in whom I am well pleased.
	2 Corinthians 13:14;	The grace of the Lord Jesus Christ, and the love of God, and the communion of the Holy Ghost, be with you all. Amen.
Holy Ghost Power	Titus 3:5;	Not by works of righteousness which we have done, but according to his mercy he saved us, by the washing of regeneration, and renewing of the Holy Ghost;
	Acts 1:8;	But ye shall receive power, after that the Holy Ghost is come upon you: and ye shall be witnesses unto me both in Jerusalem, and in all Judaea, and in Samaria, and unto the uttermost part of the earth.

IMPORTANT INFORMATION

Quick Scriptural References		
Topic	**Passage**	**Text (King James Version)**
Holy Ghost Power	Romans 8:26-27;	26 Likewise the Spirit also helpeth our infirmities: for we know not what we should pray for as we ought: but the Spirit itself maketh intercession for us with groanings which cannot be uttered. 27 And he that searcheth the hearts knoweth what is the mind of the Spirit, because he maketh intercession for the saints according to the will of God.
	Acts 2:1-4;	1 And when the day of Pentecost was fully come, they were all with one accord in one place. 2 And suddenly there came a sound from heaven as of a rushing mighty wind, and it filled all the house where they were sitting. 3 And there appeared unto them cloven tongues like as of fire, and it sat upon each of them. 4 And they were all filled with the Holy Ghost, and began to speak with other tongues, as the Spirit gave them utterance.

IMPORTANT INFORMATION

Quick Scriptural References		
Topic	Passage	Text (King James Version)
The comforter	John 14:15-18; 23;	15 If ye love me, keep my commandments. 16 And I will pray the Father, and he shall give you another Comforter, that he may abide with you for ever; 17 Even the Spirit of truth; whom the world cannot receive, because it seeth him not, neither knoweth him: but ye know him; for he dwelleth with you, and shall be in you. 18 I will not leave you comfortless: I will come to you. 23 Jesus answered and said unto him, If a man love me, he will keep my words: and my Father will love him, and we will come unto him, and make our abode with him.

Quick Scriptural References		
Topic	**Passage**	**Text (King James Version)**
The comforter	John 16:7-14;	7 Nevertheless I tell you the truth; It is expedient for you that I go away: for if I go not away, the Comforter will not come unto you; but if I depart, I will send him unto you. 8 And when he is come, he will reprove the world of sin, and of righteousness, and of judgment: 9 Of sin, because they believe not on me; 10 Of righteousness, because I go to my Father, and ye see me no more; 11 Of judgment, because the prince of this world is judged. 12 I have yet many things to say unto you, but ye cannot bear them now. 13 Howbeit when he, the Spirit of truth, is come, he will guide you into all truth: for he shall not speak of himself; but whatsoever he shall hear, that shall he speak: and he will shew you things to come. 14 He shall glorify me: for he shall receive of mine, and shall shew it unto you.

IMPORTANT INFORMATION

Quick Scriptural References		
Topic	**Passage**	**Text (King James Version)**
Holy Power	**1 Corinthians 14:2-5;**	2 For he that speaketh in an unknown tongue speaketh not unto men, but unto God: for no man understandeth him; howbeit in the spirit he speaketh mysteries. 3 But he that prophesieth speaketh unto men to edification, and exhortation, and comfort. 4 He that speaketh in an unknown tongue edifieth himself; but he that prophesieth edifieth the church. 5 I would that ye all spake with tongues but rather that ye prophesied: for greater is he that prophesieth than he that speaketh with tongues, except he interpret, that the church may receive edifying.
	Jude 1:20;	But ye, beloved, building up yourselves on your most holy faith, praying in the Holy Ghost,

97

IMPORTANT INFORMATION

Quick Scriptural References		
Topic	**Passage**	**Text (King James Version)**
Holy Baptism	**Acts 2:38-39;**	38 Then Peter said unto them, Repent, and be baptized every one of you in the name of Jesus Christ for the remission of sins, and ye shall receive the gift of the Holy Ghost. 39 For the promise is unto you, and to your children, and to all that are afar off, even as many as the LORD our God shall call.

IMPORTANT INFORMATION

Quick Scriptural References		
Topic	**Passage**	**Text (King James Version)**
Holy Ghost Baptism brings power	Luke 11:9-13;	9 And I say unto you, Ask, and it shall be given you; seek, and ye shall find; knock, and it shall be opened unto you. 10 For every one that asketh receiveth; and he that seeketh findeth; and to him that knocketh it shall be opened. 11 If a son shall ask bread of any of you that is a father, will he give him a stone? or if he ask a fish, will he for a fish give him a serpent? 12 Or if he shall ask an egg, will he offer him a scorpion? 13 If ye then, being evil, know how to give good gifts unto your children: how much more shall your heavenly Father give the Holy Spirit to them that ask him?
	Zechariah 4:6;	Then he answered and spake unto me, saying, This is the word of the LORD unto Zerubbabel, saying, Not by might, nor by power, but by my spirit, saith the LORD of hosts.
	2 Corinthians. 13:14;	The grace of the Lord Jesus Christ, and the love of God, and the communion of the Holy Ghost, be with you all. Amen.

IMPORTANT INFORMATION

Quick Scriptural References		
Topic	Passage	Text (King James Version)
The Holy Ghost leads us to our father	Romans 8:14.	For as many as are led by the Spirit of God, they are the sons of God.

IMPORTANT INFORMATION

www.ingramcontent.com/pod-product-compliance
Lightning Source LLC
LaVergne TN
LVHW091203080426
835509LV00006B/813